PROLIFIC PROFIT

HOW SUCCESSFUL BUSINESSES
MAXIMIZE PROFITS AND DOMINATE THE MARKET

MICHEL VALBRUN, CPA

AWARD-WINNING AUTHOR

Copyright & Disclaimer

This publication is designed to provide general information regarding the subject matter covered. It is not intended to serve as legal, tax, or other financial advice related to individual situations. Because each individual's legal, tax, and financial situation are different, specific advice should be tailored to their particular circumstances. For this reason, you are advised to consult with your own attorney, CPA, and/or other advisor regarding your specific situation.

The information and all accompanying material are for your use and convenience only. We have taken reasonable precautions in the preparation of this material and believe that the information presented in this material is accurate as of the date it was written. However, we will assume no responsibility for any errors or omissions. We specifically disclaim any liability resulting from the use or application of the information contained in this book.

To ensure compliance with requirements imposed by the IRS, we inform you that any US federal tax advice contained in this communication (including any attachments) is not intended or written to be used, and it cannot be used for the purpose of (i) avoiding penalties under the Internal Revenue Code or (ii) promoting, marketing, or recommending to another party any transaction or matter addressed herein. Always seek advice based on your particular circumstances from an independent advisor. Any trademarks, service marks, product names, and named features are assumed to be the property of their respective owners and are used only for reference. No endorsement is implied when we use one of these terms. Any disclosure, copying, or distribution of this material, or the taking of any action based on it, is strictly prohibited.

Published by Apex Press
Copyright © 2020 by Valbrun Group, LLC.
ISBN: 978-1-7343489-2-7

DEDICATION

To you, the courageous entrepreneur.

Table of Contents

Foreword

A s the author of 10 best-selling books, including Double Your Income Doing What You Love and Branding Small Business for Dummies™, and co-author of the New York Times Best-Seller Chicken Soup for the Parent's Soul™, I rarely come across a book quite as special as Prolific Profit™. The message of the book is simple yet important. To truly succeed in business, you MUST be prolific. To quote my dearest friend Jack Canfield, "I believe people should live full lives and not settle for anything less." This book shows you how to do just that!

In this time of economic uncertainty, the timing of this book couldn't be more perfect. Whether you are just starting out in business or run a multi-million-dollar company, any entrepreneur committed to success can benefit from the strategies shared in this book. As you will learn, success is not guaranteed—it is only achieved by those who are relentless about fulfilling their Prolific Purpose.

Over the past 40 years, I've grown several million-dollar businesses and have helped countless people do the same. If you apply the principles in this book, I have no doubt that you will dramatically change your business and transform the lives of the people around you. Using his C.P.A. Success System, Michel Valbrun teaches you how to guarantee business success through Clarity (C), Power (P), and Accountability (A) so that you can move ever closer towards living your dreams.

I wish I had a book like this when I began my entrepreneurial journey that spelled out, in plain English, how to define my purpose, set goals, read financial statements, save money on taxes, protect my assets, and create metrics to evaluate and grow my business. It would have saved me headaches, money, and more importantly, time. In Prolific Profit, Michel shares all of this information and more.

The tremendous value in this book exemplifies Michel's commitment to improving the lives of his clients. With real-world examples, along with practical business principles from some of the most successful entrepreneurs, Michel over-delivers to ensure you walk away more knowledgeable about how to maximize profits and dominate the market.

Michel, I'm truly honored that you entrusted me to be part of such excellent literary work.

Raymond Aaron
New York Times Bestselling Author

About the Author

Michel Valbrun, CPA, is an award-winning author and speaker from South Florida who studied accounting at the University of Florida. He currently lives in Atlanta with his wife Racquel.

Growing up in a single-parent household, as his father was incarcerated, Michel quickly adopted the will to succeed. Following graduation from university, he went on to become a Certified Public Accountant, starting his career with Ernst and Young, one of the largest and most prestigious professional services firms in the world. He later went to start his own firm, helping business owners maximize their profits through value-added CPA services. He is currently the President of Prolific Profit, a professional services firm with its roots in tax planning, outsourced CFO services, and financial consulting.

Michel has also been writing about finance and accountancy for many years. His work has been featured in numerous magazines and journals such as the Business News Daily, AICPA Journal of Accountancy, The Street, and more. His book, Prolific Profit: How Successful Businesses Maximize Profits and Dominate the Market, provides a blueprint for business owners to significantly improve profits and create a sustainable business.

In his free time, Michel does volunteer work and enjoys reading, attending personal development conferences, and public speaking. His dream for the future (his Prolific Purpose) is to provide financial transformations to over one million people through seminars, workshops, online courses, and professional services.

You can contact or follow Michel Valbrun at: ProlificProfit.com

LinkedIn: www.linkedin.com/in/michelvalbrun

Instagram: www.instagram.com/michelvabrun

Facebook: www.facebook.com/michelvalbrun

YouTube: www.youtube.com/c/michelvalbrun

Twitter: www.twitter.com/michelvalbrun

Prolific Preface: Get Rich or Die Tryin'

Facedown and laid out on my living room floor, I could feel the cold steel of two loaded guns pointed at my head. I was ten years old, living in Miami, Florida, with my mom, two sisters, my aunt, and some visiting relatives. As usual, I have been patiently waiting for my mom to come home from a long day of work. I was particularly eager to tell her all about my day at school because I had just finished what I believed to be the most beautiful family portrait ever painted. I waited for her by the door, and I got excited the moment I heard her car pull up outside.

As the door cracked open, my mom's demeanor seemed different than usual. She didn't look happy to see me, and her face was full of fear. Instead of greeting me with the usual hug and two kisses, she looked me dead in the eyes. "Go, Michel," she said in a dull monotone.

As she took a few more careful steps into the house, and the image of an unfamiliar man followed behind her. I squinted my eyes to see if I could recognize this stranger, but after she took a few more steps, I could see the gun pressed into the back of my mother's head. It wasn't my first time seeing a gun, because my dad used to carry a handgun around the house. In those days, I was extremely vocal and used to get in trouble in class for my hyperactive behavior, but something told me that this wasn't the time to speak up. I backed up from the front door on the balls of my feet, not saying a word.

As my mother continued to make her way into the house, my uncle, who was visiting us from Haiti, quietly followed behind her. Another gunman poking a gun into his back unpleasantly escorted my uncle inside the house. A third and fourth gunman appeared, each one dressed from head-to-toe in black. The first gunman said in Creole, "Tell the boy to get on the floor." My mom repeated the instructions back to me in English, and I nervously came back into the living room and laid down on the cold floor.

The first gunman then told my mom to gather everyone in the house and ask them to do the same. As my family members entered the living room, I could hear confusion and fear echo throughout the room. My grandmother, who was also visiting from Haiti, was asked to lie down as well.

As I laid on the floor, I could hear a gunman kick my uncle and shout in Creole, "Where's the money? Where's the money?" I then heard my mom shout: "He doesn't know! I will show you where it is." Back then, my parents' idea of a money management system was an old shoebox and envelopes full of cash. It was clear these gunmen knew this and were on a mission to get every dollar they could.

My mom directed one of the gunmen to a shoebox with the wad of paper bills, while the other three stayed in the living room to make sure we all stayed on

the floor. A few minutes later, my mom and the gunman came back with what looked like hundreds of dollars in cash stuffed in white envelopes.

As the gunmen fled back into the night, my family sat there in silence, traumatized by what had just unfolded. As I approached my mother, shaking in fear, the only comforting words she was able to share were, "We're lucky. They usually kill us after they take the money."

That was a defining moment in my life. Other than the fact I could have been murdered right alongside my family, it began to shape the way I viewed

6

money. Up until that point, I saw money as a tool to buy things like toys, clothes, and food. I didn't realize the extreme measures that some people were willing to take to get these pieces of paper—things like being willing to kill for it, or risking imprisonment or even death to get their hands on it. Before I even became a teenager, I had witnessed my dad get arrested, go on house arrest, get incarcerated, and eventually get deported out of the country.

This experience ultimately forced my mother to raise three children on her own while also worrying about our family's safety. Between all these experiences, I knew that I wanted to become financially successful—and do so legally (abiding by the laws) and ethically (not compromising my values). I promised myself that once I achieved this goal, I would share my knowledge with the world. This book is the fulfillment of that promise.

What's Good?

How's business going? If you're like most small business owners, your knee jerk reaction to that question is a quick "good!" Which isn't any more honest than the burnt-out nine-to-fiver saying they're "good" on a Monday morning. On the surface, these four letters may not seem like much, but if you listen closely, this response speaks volumes. For starters, most businesses are not doing "good"; in reality, they're not even doing "okay". According to data from the U.S. Bureau of Labor Statistics, about 20 percent of new businesses fail in their first year, about 50 percent fail in their fifth year, and over 70 percent of businesses fail before 10 years have come and gone. [1] This automatic "good" response is the business equivalent of 93 percent of Americans believing they drive better than average when, statistically speaking, only 50 percent can drive better than the average. Secondly, due to the ever-increasing competition in the global market, the commoditization of goods and services, and an overcrowded marketplace, "good" is rapidly becoming not good enough. In fact, within the next few years, "good" may become the new slang for "good-bye business".

The purpose of this book is to give you clear and practical methods to transform your "good" business into a "prolific" business by achieving Prolific Profit™. Warren Buffett once stated that General Motors was a good

---

[1] https://www.fundera.com/blog/what-percentage-of-small-businesses-fail

company—and that was the problem. As you will see in this book, being a "good" company will likely be written all over your business obituary. If you want to succeed, you must be Prolific.

Throughout this book, I will define what it means to have a Prolific business, but for now, let's define Prolific Profit as the ability to generate an abundant amount of wealth for your business that will lead to market domination. Within the pages of this book, I'm not going to throw around fancy words or try to impress you with my accounting knowledge. I've intentionally written this book in a way that can be easily understood by the aspiring entrepreneur but still be transformational to the seven-figure mogul.

You will walk away with the clarity you need to achieve your Prolific Purpose, the power you need to make informed business decisions, and the accountability you need to guarantee your success. I will share with you fundamental business principles and proven best practices from some of the most successful businesses in the world. I will provide real-world examples and share with you my own personal business experience to help you apply these principles to your own business.

Throughout the book, I will provide "Reflections & Actions," which is a list of questions and actions to reinforce the material provided in the chapter. The valuable information contained in this book will do you no good if you don't

reflect on how it applies to your business or if you don't take the necessary action to change your life. If possible, I encourage you to read it with a business partner, friend, or spouse to increase your likelihood of success even further. Additionally, I've included an index so you can use the book as a reference if you ever get stuck during your journey.

By the time you finish reading this book, you will have absolute mastery over your business finances and will be fully equipped to achieve Prolific Profit.

You did not get into business to be small or to fail. So, right now, I'm not concerned with "how business is going." My only question to you right now is: "Are you ready?"

CHAPTER 1

Death of the Bean Counter

'm not your average accountant. To tell you the truth, I have a love/hate relationship with other accountants, not so much because of their quirky personalities (and I admit I have my fair share of quirks), but because of the way we've allowed ourselves to be negatively perceived by business owners.

The roots of accounting date back to ancient Mesopotamia and are closely related to developments in writing, counting, and money.[2] In 1494, Luca Pacioli, recognized as the father of modern accounting and bookkeeping, was the first person to publish a work on double-entry bookkeeping[3] (which we will discuss later). Even 500 years later, this brilliant system is the most commonly used method today because it accounts for all transaction types.

Financial statements are prepared in accordance with generally accepted accounting principles (GAAP), which include:

- Recognition: The items that should be recognized in the financial statements (for example as assets, liabilities, revenues, and expenses).

---

[2] Henio, Edrian. 1992. "Accounting Numbers as 'inscription': Action at a Distance and the Development of Accounting." Accounting, Organizations and Society 17 (7): 685–708.

[3] Heeffer, Albrecht (November 2009). "On the curious historical coincidence of algebra and double-entry bookkeeping"

- Measurement: Amounts should be reported for each of the elements included in financial statements.
- Presentation: The line items, subtotals, and totals that should be displayed in the financial statements and the way they might be aggregated within the financial statements.
- Disclosure: The specific information that is most important to the users of the financial statements. Disclosures both supplement and explain amounts in the statements.

As great as it is to have GAAP, you will learn (if you don't know already) that this system was not designed to serve you as a business owner; rather, it was designed to focus on the users of the financial statements, such as investors, creditors, management, and regulators. Many business owners struggle with the complexities of GAAP and heavily rely on their accountant to document their financials according to these principles.

This overreliance leaves business owners unaware of what's going on in their business because their accountant either doesn't explain it to them in a simple way or doesn't redirect their focus to the numbers that matter.

As a result, business owners end up spending tens of thousands of dollars each year on accounting and bookkeeping, and all they get is a bunch of financial statements, tax returns, and headaches as they try to figure out where all their money went.

By definition, "business" refers to the organized efforts and activities of individuals to produce and sell goods and services for profit. No one goes into business to be unprofitable, yet the startling statistics show that many business owners experience this unfortunate outcome:

- 33 percent of businesses fail in their first two years in business[4]
- Less than 70 percent make it to year ten (some believe the number is closer to 90 percent)
- Less than 25 percent of businesses make more than $250,000 in gross revenue[5]
- Less than 7 percent of businesses make more than $1,000,000 in gross revenue[4]

By definition, "accountants" are people who keep or inspect financial accounts. As a business owner, you may see this function as a commodity service, and as a former "bean counter," an accountant that concentrates solely on accounting at the expense of the bigger picture, I could understand why you would feel that way.

When I first started my career, I believed my only job was to organize transactions, provide financial reports, and complete tax returns as accurately as possible. While I had mastered these tasks, I felt that there was a lot more that I could do for my clients. Ultimately, I did not feel fulfilled because deep down inside I wanted to have a greater impact on businesses.

After working on what felt like the millionth tax return, I knew that I had to make a change if I wanted to make a bigger impact on the world. I began researching and seeking out some of the most successful business experts, both in and out of accounting, in order to transform the way I was doing business. Through a lot of hard work and perseverance, I can honestly say that I've cracked the code of providing superior service to my clients and helping other accountants do the same. The transformation has been nothing short of phenomenal and it has been constantly reflected in the results I provide to my clients. One of my mentors told me that "the value that you

---

[4] https://www.businessknowhow.com/startup/business-failure.htm
[5] https://www.businessknowhow.com/money/earn.htm

provide to your clients is measured in how much more the same client pays you in comparison to other people in your industry." While some accountants claim to provide high value accounting services, if they are not helping you maximize profits, it's "just a cost of doing business" and reflected in their compensation.

As you will learn in this book, there are no line items on financial statements called the "cost of doing business," and even if there were, you need those expenses to be razor thin. As it stands, accounting departments are considered just a "cost center". If you're not familiar, a cost center is a department of a company that takes care of the costs of that department. On the other hand, a "profit center" is a department of a company that is responsible for revenues, profits, and costs. Given that accountants are the ones who are closest to profit, because they see all the transactions of the business, they are in a unique position to drive the most value to businesses. In fact, I believe we have a fiduciary duty of actively working with business owners to help increase profits instead of operating as a costly unavoidable business function.

One of the reasons businesses achieve prolific profit is they make sure that they only spend on "investments" in their business. Just think about it for a moment. Why else would you spend money on your business? There should only be two reasons: To grow revenue or decrease expenses. That's it!

Every penny you spend in your business must be an investment (except for tax) that either grows revenues or eliminates wasteful expenses. Money spent that does not support one of these two outcomes is money flushed down the toilet. However, I have great news for you: All investments earn a return, and all returns can be measured! By measuring your accountant's ability to either help you increase revenue or decrease unnecessary expenses, you can quickly quantify the value they're truly providing.

All Accountants Aren't Created Equal

As a recovering bean counter, I've found that there are some key differences between accountants. Unfortunately, many businesses see all accountants as the same, which couldn't be further from the truth. The main types of accountants are:

- Bookkeeper: Keeps records of the financial affairs of a business.
- Accountant: Keeps or inspects financial accounts with an undergraduate degree in accounting.
- Tax Preparer: Calculates, files, and signs income tax returns on behalf of individuals and businesses.
- Enrolled Agent (EA): Federally authorized tax practitioner empowered by the U.S. Department of the Treasury.
- Certified Public Accountant (CPA): An accounting professional who has passed the Uniform CPA examination and has also met additional state certification and experience requirements.

Just as with practitioners in the medical field, an accountant's education, training, experience, legal rights, and results vary a great deal. Putting all accountants in one bucket is like thinking the eight-year-old playing Hasbro's Operation is the same as a brain surgeon. I believe there are five distinguishing factors among accountants that separate the good from the Prolific:

- **Education:** This relates to the level of accounting and tax knowledge acquired through high school and college. You'll be surprised to learn that bookkeepers and tax preparers are not required to have any upper-level qualifications, such as a bachelor's degree. It's terrifying that big chain tax companies such as H&R Block and Jackson Hewitt will hire practically anyone to do your business taxes. In fact, according to H&R Block's website, the only requirement they have is that "students must be 18 years of age to attend their Income Tax Course (a GED or diploma, however, is not required) and pass the course."[6]

- **Legal Authority:** If you have a tax problem, a notice from the IRS, or are under audit, you will need someone to represent you before the IRS. This representation is only granted to CPAs, enrolled agents, or tax attorneys, and only these individuals are able to "take your place" in front of the IRS. Representation at the IRS is essential if you are audited. This valuable service can give you some serious peace of mind.

- **Training:** For CPAs, this is known as continuing professional education (CPE). It is a requirement that is designed to help maintain their competency and skill sets as providers of professional services. To maintain their license, a CPA must have 120 CPE credit hours with a three-year span.

- **Experience:** This relates to the type of work experience that an accountant has. In the accounting profession, the main categories of work experience include accounting (keep or inspect financial accounts), tax (determine the amount of money owed to federal, state, or local agencies), and audit (examination of financial records). CPAs are required to pass a four-part exam covering all these topics but don't necessarily specialize in all these categories. In addition to the main types of accounting experience, accountants could be self-employed, or they could work in either a small or large business. Many accountants who have worked at the "The Big 4" accounting firms—KPMG, Ernst & Young (EY), Deloitte, and PricewaterhouseCoopers (PwC)—have experience working with several of the largest companies in the world. The Big 4 accounting firms serve 99% of the Fortune 1,000 companies[7]. While this may not

---

[6] https://www.hrblock.com/tax-center/around-block/become-tax-preparer/
[7] https://big4accountingfirms.com/

seem important to you, I believe success leaves clues. Having someone on your team who has seen how many of the largest companies in the world operate can help your business achieve that status as well.

- **Bottom Line (Results):** More important than all of these categories are results. There's no use hiring an overeducated, trained-up, experienced accountant if he or she can't produce the results you are looking for in your business. Results are the bottom-line criteria. You are better off hiring an accountant with none of the above criteria so long as they are producing results. The results that an individual produces should be the single most crucial factor in deciding whom you work with. Someone with a proven track record, whether through testimonials or case studies (what I call "receipts"), can significantly grow your business or provide an immediate return on investment for the business owner.

The State of Business vs. The Profit-Producing Professional

In order to achieve prolific profit, your company needs a dramatic change and new breed of professional, who checks all the above-mentioned boxes and more: Someone who can take your business from "good" (i.e., trending towards failure) to prolific (i.e., trending towards success). I call this

individual the profit-producing professional (PPP); someone who has a way of thinking that enables them to walk into any business, gauge its current financial status, and clearly define the problems that the owner is facing. They are then able to determine specific and detailed action steps that are needed to arrive at a solution. Not only that, they know how to implement and monitor the solution on an ongoing basis so that they can hold management accountable for achieving those goals. In short, bean counters count the beans while PPPs create **more** beans.

As a PPP, I constantly identify ways to add value to my clients' businesses. In fact, many of my clients call me "Money Makin' Mich" for this very reason.

Along with the technical skills and abilities of a PPP, they have the following personality traits:

- Passionate about growing revenues and eliminating the unnecessary expenses (unlike the typical accountant who is passionate about recording these transactions).
- Highly skilled and significantly proactive when it comes to reducing taxes for the business owner (unlike the accountant who reactively reduces taxes during tax season).
- Well-connected with a vast network of trusted advisors (unlike the quiet, anti-social accountant).
- Obsessed with identifying opportunities for you to achieve prolific profit (legally and ethically).
- Can easily communicate with and educate their clients in accounting and tax matters (unlike the ego-driven accountant who throws around fancy accounting language not used by most entrepreneurs).
- Earns more (or saves more) money than you're paying them (the true definition of investment).

If your current accountant is missing any of the above criteria, it may be worth considering either replacing them or adding a PPP to your team to supplement the areas they are missing, even for a shorter-term project such as helping you save $10,000 to $100,000 in taxes legally and ethically (my core principles as mentioned in the Prolific Preface). If you ever come across a PPP, they will be able to quickly rattle off a list of things they've done to add value to clients. For example:

- Through our strategic tax plan, we were able to save ABC company $27,541 in taxes this year and every year going forward.

- I've referred seven clients to my current client's business since the beginning of the year, generating over $165,000 in new sales.
- I've identified how a top sales guy was stealing over $23,500 in commissions due to a lack of controls in the business.
- I've recommended a new customer relationship management (CRM) system which increased our client's close rates by 23%.

While it may appear that I compete with other accountants, the services I provide to my clients are uniquely designed for their specific needs. Therefore, I proactively partner with other accountants to enable them to provide even more value to their clients. I've also found that some accountants are extremely passionate about the traditional accounting work but prefer to partner with someone else who can identify new ways of helping their clients.

Hopefully, you get the point by now. I believe accountants have the ability to provide a tremendous amount of value to business owners, but unfortunately the vast majority of accountants struggled like I once did because many of these concepts I share in this book are not taught in schools, even at the university level. It's not only a call to action for business owners to change their expectations of what the accounting department can do for their business, it's also a wakeup call for accountants to rethink the way they can proactively add value instead of allowing business owners to believe they are a drag on the bottom line.

To be clear, I have a high degree of respect for all accountants. The service we provide for business owners is essential. In fact, some of my closest personal and business relationships are with accountants in all of these categories. They all have unique skill sets, strengths, capabilities, and a handful of them fit into the PPP category. On the other hand, there are other accountants that are not committed to helping their client's business succeed. Every time I allow a customer or client to walk away without working with me, I know deep down that the risk of their business failing significantly increases. Moreover, as a business owner, that's how you need to feel about the product or service you deliver in the market.

I suggest that "we" accountants commit ourselves to deliver value (return on investment) to everyone we come in contact with, whether that's investing in yourself through trainings or partnering with a PPP. This doesn't make me any better than the other amazing accountants who are in pursuit of helping their client's business. Like a successful sports team, my passion and unique ability to step into a business, educate my clients on the actions that need to be taken, and let the accountant do what they do best, will improve the chances of success.

As you will learn, domination in the market requires constant evaluation and improvement. As a PPP, I hold myself to the very same standards. If working with me doesn't produce a measurable and demonstrable ROI for your business every three to six months, then I don't deserve to be paid, and I most certainly deserve to get fired. No explanations, no excuses, no apologies. Plain and simple.

Reflections & Action

1. What value-added services does your current accountant provide (if any)?

   _____

2. How much has your current accountant increased your profits?

   _____

3. What is your plan for replacing your current accountant or adding a PPP to your team?

   _____

CHAPTER 2

A New Paradigm for CPA

In the traditional sense, a Certified Public Accountant (CPA) is the customary title of qualified accountants in numerous countries. In the United States, a CPA is licensed to provide accounting services to the public. As a CPA, I have tremendous respect for all the professionals that have achieved this title because of the level of effort required in order to obtain those three letters. I believe that all successful business owners need an exceptional CPA on their team to achieve Prolific Profits ... but not just any CPA.

As we discussed in the previous chapter, a Profit Producing Professional (PPP) is a new type of accountant that proactively adds value to the business either individually or with other professionals. As a PPP, my objective is to provide business owners with a system to significantly increase profitability and drive overall business success. Those three letters, C-P-A, do a great job at explaining "what" I do: yes, I'm "Certified," meaning I passed a painstakingly long four-part exam; yes, I'm "Public," meaning I offer my services in an open market; yes, I'm an "Accountant" with over 150 college credit hours and an additional 40 hours I must take every year called continuing education credits, along with ethical standards and practices I must abide by. Additionally, I'm technically proficient

in general accounting matters such as financial statements, business transactions, taxes, and business law.

But while this is all great, it doesn't explain why it matters to you, the business owner. What can I say when a business owner asks me: "Why do I need you?"

Based on my experience working with countless businesses and entrepreneurs, I've cracked the code of communicating the true value that I and other Profit Producing Professionals provide to business owners. This system encapsulates what I believe to be my professional duty as a CPA, which I call the CPA Success System. The CPA Success System consists of three different components: Clarity, Power, and Accountability.

C.P.A. SUCCESS SYSTEM

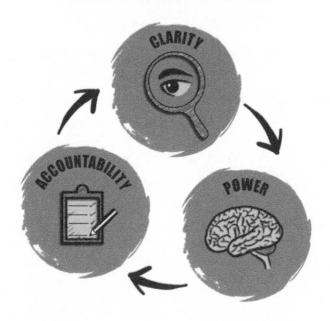

Clarity (C)

The first component of the CPA Success System is Clarity. Clarity is defined as the quality of being coherent and intelligible. Synonyms for the word clarity include clearness, simplicity, precision, and transparency.

The reason why this is important for business owners is that many entrepreneurs are not even clear on why they're in business in the first place. Far too many business owners have either gone into business to be "financially free" or to be "their own boss". While these may be worthwhile goals, these are not powerful enough to make you want to wake up every day and dominate the market.

You don't need to have all the steps perfectly laid out, but by being clear on your destination, you can pivot and adjust your actions along the way. When an airplane takes off, they are off course 99% of the time. The role of the pilot is to continually bring the plane back on course so that it arrives on schedule to its destination. As the pilot of your business, you must do the same.

As you'll also learn in this book, your purpose should be customer-centric. Your purpose does not need to be overly complex. In fact, the simpler it is, the easier it will be for you to stay focused and communicate your message.

Take, for instance, the beginnings of the most profitable airline, Southwest. As many great business stories start off, Rollin King and Herb Kelleher created Southwest Airlines more than 40 years ago on a cocktail napkin. [8]King and Kelleher went to a restaurant in San Antonio and ordered drinks. Rollin then grabbed a cocktail napkin, took out his pen, and said to Kelleher, "Here's the plan." He then drew a simple triangle on the napkin. At the apex of the triangle, he wrote Dallas. The bottom left, he labeled San Antonio. On

---

8   https://www.inc.com/bill-murphy-jr/southwest-airlines-co-founder-ceo-herb-kelleher-has-died-this-1-story-explains-his-amazing-leadership-style.html

the bottom right, he wrote Houston. He said, "There – that's the business plan. Fly between these cities several times a day, every day." And that is the story of how Southwest Airlines began, on a simple napkin in a bar in San Antonio. There is a plaque proudly displayed at the Southwest Airlines headquarters that enshrines a version of the original napkin. This one simple notion: If you get your passengers to their destinations when they want to get there, on time, at the lowest possible fares, and make darn sure they have a good time doing it, people will fly your airline. And you know what? They were right.

By being clear on your destination, you'll be able to achieve your goals and maintain that success despite challenging economic times. By having clarity about what really matters, you will be clear about what doesn't matter.

Power (P)

The next portion of the CPA Success System is Power. My favorite definition of power is the capacity or ability to direct or influence the behavior of others or the course of events. By first gaining clarity, you become clear on what it is you want to accomplish, which gives you the power to influence and direct the course of events.

For instance, in this book I will discuss the value-added PPP service of tax planning. If you're not familiar (don't worry, the vast majority aren't implementing it yet), tax planning is the analysis of your business and

personal life to significantly increase your tax efficiency. Tax efficiency minimizes tax liability when given many different financial decisions. A financial decision is said to be tax efficient if the tax outcome is lower than an alternative financial structure that achieves the same end. Therefore, by going through an analysis of your business and life with a PPP, you will have the knowledge (which will in turn give you the power) to significantly reduce your tax liability and increase profits.

Let me be clear, there is a big difference between tax evasion and tax avoidance. Tax evasion is the illegal non-payment or underpayment of tax, whereas tax avoidance is the arrangement of one's financial affairs to minimize tax liability within the law.

American judge and judicial philosopher Learned Hand once said, "Anyone may so arrange his affairs that his taxes shall be as low as possible; he is not bound to choose that pattern which will best pay the Treasury. There is not even a patriotic duty to increase one's taxes." [9] Otherwise, you must pay taxes, but it's also foolish to believe that you must leave a tip by overpaying.

A great example of this is a recent client of mine who was overpaying in taxes by over $43,000. Through analysis of his business and life, I identified several deductions his current CPA was not maximizing, deductible business expenses he was not tracking because he did not know they were deductible, and ways to shift income to a lower tax bracket. We set up the business in the most tax-efficient entity to avoid paying unnecessary taxes.

Assuming the business owner decides to take those annual tax savings and put them into a retirement account averaging a 12% rate of return for 32 years, by the time they retire at age 67 their investment account would've grown to $13,304,228. Now that's POWER!

Accountability (A)

Once you've acquired this power, you must apply it. This brings us to the A in the CPA Success System, which represents Accountability. Robert T. Kiyosaki, the author of Rich Dad, Poor Dad, says, "The word accounting comes from the word accountability. If you are going to be rich, you need to be accountable for your money." While many businesses are very good at

---

[9] https://www.uschamber.com/above-the-fold/the-president-vs-learned-hand

identifying their goals and gaining knowledge, what virtually guarantees business success is accountability. Without accountability, humans tend to fall to their vices. As you'll see in this book, the most successful entrepreneurs have all implemented systems to remain accountable enough to consistently generate and improve their success. I'll share all about the benefits about having accountability, but for now I'll introduce how a lack of accountability can hurt your business.

Many business owners are unfortunately oblivious to the impending demise of their business. One of the biggest reasons why business owners believe they're doing "good" is because they have nothing or no one to warn them when they are off track. Since many business owners are not actively looking at their financials, they have no idea how well they are performing. Even the ones that do look at their financials don't fully understand them or have

nothing in place to let them know how well they're doing. It's like playing a game of basketball without a scoreboard. Sure, you may see one team getting the ball into the basket more often than another team, but this doesn't necessarily mean they're winning. If you have one team hitting 50 two-pointers (100 points) vs. another team shooting 35 three-pointers (105 points), on the surface it may look the team getting the ball in the hoop 50 times is winning, but the scoreboard will reveal that that hot-shooting team is really losing by five points.

By applying this system, you'll quickly find that your business success will grow at exponential rates. The system is designed to be an iterative process and therefore, must be repeated over and over again. As you cycle through the system, your gains grow with each iteration.

Reflections & Actions

1. Do you currently have an accountant that you're working with, and if so, do they fit the model of the old accountant or the new accountant?

_____

2. What portion of the CPA Success System do you think you need the most help with?

_____

PART I

CLARITY

CHAPTER 3

To Be Or Not To Be (Prolific): Prolific Or Perish

⸻

"To be, or not to be" is the opening phrase in Act 3, Scene 1 in William Shakespeare's *Hamlet*. In the speech, Hamlet contemplates death and suicide, trying to decide whether it's worth enduring the pain and unfairness of life while also acknowledging that the alternative might be worse. The struggles and financial woes of owning your own business can lead some entrepreneurs down the same demoralizing path, and many reach a point where they contemplate whether they should try to resurrect a dying business or kill it off altogether.

There are major external factors, such as the national and global economies, that can significantly impact the rise or fall of a business. Historically, economic contractions occur every ten years. Some contractions happen sooner than the ten-year window, and some are bigger or last longer than the ones before it, but the pattern remains generally the same. I often like to think about the economy as an ocean of opportunity. When the tide is up (economic expansion), everyone is happy, swimming, and joyful. In business, this could mean increases in revenue, staff, and market share. When the tide is low (economic contraction), everyone is scared, angry, and broke. As the tide gets lower, panic begins to set in. Studies also show that the suicide rate increases six months before a rise in unemployment[10]. Billionaire investor Warren Buffet has said that: "Only when the tide goes out do you discover who's been swimming naked."

This quote brings clarity to the previously mentioned statistic that only 33% of businesses survive past the ten-year mark. What this shows is that the businesses that were successful during a rising tide (expansion) were only riding the wave of a good economy. Think back on all the money made during the dot-com boom in the late 90s or the real estate riches from 2003–2007. When the tide disappeared, so did the riches.

To be considered truly successful in business, you must maintain success despite fluctuations in the economy. Your "championship" game match isn't against those who you believe are your competitors. The true opponents are the economy and your lack of commitment to achieving Prolific Profits. Many business owners approach business as a sprint, thinking that the fastest growth wins the race. But from my experience, business is more of a marathon than a sprint, which is more about endurance than speed. In order to be sustainable, it should no longer be acceptable to be "good" to build a successful business. The only way to be successful in business is to be prolific. By being prolific, you become highly productive in creating cash flow. By definition, productivity is the effectiveness of effort, as measured in terms of the rate of output per unit of input. Therefore, productivity is not a measure of speed, but output. According to Paul J. Meyer, considered to be the pioneer of the self-improvement industry, productivity is never an accident. It is always the result of a commitment to excellence, intelligent planning, and focused effort.

---

[10] https://www.ncbi.nlm.nih.gov/pmc/articles/PMC3423193/

Michel's Hierarchy of Business Success

The famous American psychologist, Abraham Harold Maslow, created the widely respected Maslow's hierarchy of needs, which is a theory of psychological health that focuses on the prioritization of human needs. In Maslow's hierarchy of needs, he used the terms "physiological, safety, belonging and love," "social needs," "esteem," and "self-actualization" to describe the general evolution of human needs. Each level has its own unique attributes and characteristics. To step up to the next level, the previous level must be satisfied. The goal is to get to the top of the hierarchy of needs.

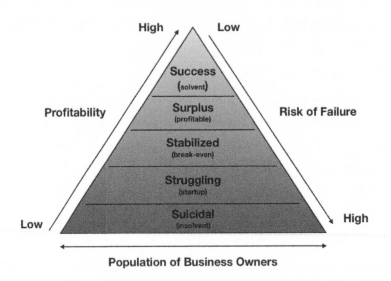

By adapting Maslow's scheme to the business world, I've created (which hopefully will be famously known) Michel's Hierarchy of Business Success. I believe that there are five levels of business success (or lack thereof). These five levels from lowest to highest are "suicidal," "struggling/startup," "stabilized," "surplus," and "success".

#	Level	Characteristics	Financial Indicators
1	Suicidal	Consistent losses and negative cash flow with minimal opportunity to recover. Inability to pay expenses and debts. Likely to face bankruptcy.	Negative profits, negative cash flow.
2	Struggling	Losses and inconsistent cash flow or first year in business. Risk of facing bankruptcy.	More negative profits and cash flow than positive.
3	Stabilized	Breakeven in an expanding economy. Risk of operating at a loss.	Little to no difference in profit or cash flow.
4	Surplus	Profitable in an expanding economy.	Positive profits and cash flow.
5	Success	Profitable in ALL economies.	High profits, high cash flow.

Much like Maslow's Hierarchy of Needs, each level must be satisfied before moving to the next. The entry point for all businesses is the startup/struggling level. For first-year entrepreneurs, this could be the make-or-break point for your business since it will set the tone of how you will operate. By definition, an entrepreneur is a person who organizes and operates a business or businesses, and they frequently take on greater than normal financial risks to do so.

It is important to note that all levels below "success" are contingent on an expanding economy; the "success" level can only be revealed in a contracting economy. Being profitable now may mean that you have a successful business during a rising tide, but you can very quickly get knocked down to insolvency when the market contracts.

Take a look at the last great recession we had. In early 2006, the United States housing bubble and subprime mortgage crisis shattered the value of homes and decimated retirement funds. Before the crisis, everyone involved in the real estate industry was getting overly rich for no other reason than an inflated housing market. The so-called "successes" achieved by financial institutions, realtors, and real estate investors quickly evaporated once the market corrected and only the truly successful survived the collapse.

In the accounting world, we use a term called "going concern." A going concern is a business that functions without the threat of liquidation for the foreseeable future, which is usually regarded as at least the next 12 months. In my opinion, the only true going concern in the Hierarchy of Business Needs is the highest level: "success."

By definition, the word prolific means plentiful, or something available in large quantities. Some synonyms for the word prolific include abundance, bountiful, and rich. The word profit is defined as a financial gain, especially the difference between the amount earned and the amount spent in buying, operating, or producing something. In business terms, this is the highest level of the Hierarchy of Business Needs. To reach this level requires

following the C.P.A. Success System, which provides a direct path to achieving this goal. The first step to being truly Prolific in business is to have a Prolific Purpose.

Reflections & Actions

1. How long have you been in business and how long do you expect your business to be around?

   _____

2. Based on Michel's Hierarchy of Business Success, what level do you believe your business is in?

   _____

3. What is your current profit and cash flow? What action can you take today to increase those numbers?

   _____

CHAPTER 4

What is Your Prolific Purpose?

The word purpose is defined as the reason for which something is done or created. Synonyms for this word include: motive, motivation, cause, reason, and justification. If we combine the words Prolific and Purpose using the definitions presented above, a Prolific Purpose can be thought of as a cause with abundant possibilities. To explain further, the only restriction to your Prolific Purpose is your imagination. By positioning your Prolific Purpose powerfully, you will be in a position to consistently be aligned to your mission and execute your goals.

The path of entrepreneurship is not an easy road. I have tremendous amount of respect for anyone who pursues an entrepreneurial path. One of the things that has helped me during my entrepreneurial journey is having a Prolific Purpose—or, to put it another way, a *Why*. Though you may have intuitively stumbled across a few ideas—such as "to have more money," "to be my own boss," "to help more people," or "to take care of my family"—many entrepreneurs have problems succinctly defining their Why.

In his book *Start With Why*, Simon Sinek explains, "You need to know your own WHY and be able to articulate that WHY in simple, clear terms. [11]For Apple, it's 'Think different.' For Southwest Airlines, it's to be the champion for the common man and to make air travel accessible to all. Bob Iger, CEO of

---

[11] https://medium.com/leadership-motivation-and-impact/the-power-of-starting-with-why-f8e491392ef8

Disney, boils down their WHY to, 'We're in the business of telling stories.'" By defining your Prolific Purpose, you will be magnetized towards your goals which will then attract all the people that your business will help. As Sinek also wrote, "People don't buy WHAT you do; they buy WHY you do it."

More importantly, in the pursuit of your Prolific Purpose, you become an even more significant contribution to the world. Much like the safety instructions on an airplane when they tell you to put your mask on first before you can begin assisting others, the same philosophy applies to achieving your Prolific Purpose. If you're not clear on your Prolific Purpose (your oxygen), then your chances of helping someone else (their oxygen mask) is low.

It is not enough to have a profitable business. This will only take care of necessities such as food, shelter, clothing, maybe a nice car and some vacations. By achieving your Prolific Purpose, you can make a bigger contribution to your family, friends, community, and the world. Your Prolific Purpose is your duty, responsibility, and moral obligation.

Crafting Your Prolific Purpose

If you've been alive for any period of time, you've likely confronted some challenges. Chances are, without consciously thinking about it, you had a WHY that drove you to overcome that challenge. Whether it was your children, your aspiration to achieve financial freedom, the impact you can make in the world, or even to survive, your WHY gave you the motivation you needed to see it through.

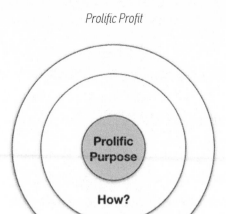

Similarly, a Prolific Purpose allows you to concentrate your efforts on what matters. It's what empowers you to take risks and push ahead no matter the obstacles that are in your path. Humans are wired differently than animals; animals are driven by survival, while humans are driven to have more in life.

Understanding your Prolific Purpose is a significant initial step in figuring out what goals excite you and make you feel alive. There are several books and

methods about finding your purpose, giving you a more in-depth insight into what drives you, but for now let's start with the basics:

1. What excites you?

Whenever you're working toward things that inspire you, you start to feel alive. For me, I'm passionate about entrepreneurship and the challenges that come along with it. Growing up, I was into video games, and one of my favorite games was The Sims. I loved how I was able to create and build an entire world. I would spend hours playing the game to see the impact of the things I added and removed. Entrepreneurship gives me this same excitement, which is why I love it so much. Your Prolific Purpose should be something you are excited about which you can then link to a cause that is bigger than yourself.

2. What are your values?

Your values don't necessarily need to be tied to money, but it's essential to recognize what's most important to you. For instance, do you value your family, amusement, balance, or generosity? What about comfort, independence, justice, creativity, leadership, or love? Or maybe it's energy, equality, productivity, security, significance, spirituality, success, trust, wealth, or wisdom? I recommend that you take a few moments to identify what you truly value. Your values will also act as a guardrail on your entrepreneurial journey. Based on some of the life experiences I shared in

my Prolific Preface, I highly value achieving financial success legally and ethically.

3. Where would you add the best value?

It's one thing to be passionate about something, but it's far more effective to be passionate about something you're good at. Unfortunately, business is a competitive sport. The market doesn't care that I was passionate about The Sims growing up, nor does it care that I'm passionate about entrepreneurship. What the market cares most about is "what's in it for me?" For me, I chose accounting because it's a non-negotiable aspect of running a business, whether you learn it on your own or outsource it. My skills in accounting are valuable in the marketplace, and because I apply the C.P.A. Success System with my clients, that value is amplified. Try to find some alignment with your passion and your skills. As a business owner, you may have already identified your skills and may currently be in business doing this thing. However, as you evolve in business and life, I believe it's always a worthwhile exercise to reassess the value you bring to the world. One excellent resource to reevaluate your skills is to take a personality test. There are hundreds of tests out there, but I found the 16 Personalities test to be particularly accurate.[12]

Nevertheless, understanding your best strengths and where you can add the most value—through the use of your education, abilities, wisdom, and expertise—will help you concentrate on the opportunities, functions, and

career paths where you're most likely to succeed and, consequently, locate the best sense of achievement and participation.

The Prolific Purpose Protocol

As big as a Prolific Purpose may sound, it does not need to be all that long. The shorter, the better—it will be easier for you to remember and easier for someone to be touched, moved, and inspired by it. I've found the best format for a Prolific Purpose is the following:

My Prolific Purpose is to by

Here's mine:

> *"My Prolific Purpose is to create financial transformations for over one million people by providing clarity, power, and accountability to business owners through education and professional services."*

---

[12] https://www.16personalities.com/free-personality-test

That's it! Don't overcomplicate it.

Be sure to use the questions above as a guide to developing your Prolific Purpose. *You can download your free detailed full-color version of the Prolific Purpose template at ProlificProfit.com.*

Reflections & Action

1. Why did you get into business?

_____

2. What were the results of your personality test? How are you going to use this information in your business and your life?

_____

3. What is your Prolific Purpose?

_____

CHAPTER 5

The Billion-Dollar Word

Two of the most respected business owners in the world are Bill Gates and Warren Buffet. They have both achieved the coveted billionaire status, but what's even more impressive is how they've been able to continue to grow their businesses and their wealth despite economic contractions. When Bill Gates first met Warren Buffet, Gates' mother asked everyone around the table to identify what they believed was the most critical factor in their success through life. Without communicating with one another, both

Gates and Buffett gave the same one-word answer: "Focus."

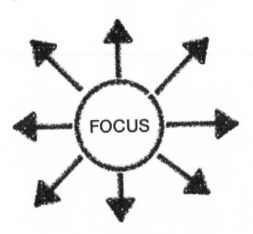

We often overestimate our ability to multitask and take on multiple things. Our cognitive ability, meaning our ability to process thoughts, is not infinite. For instance, if you were to draw your brain as a circle with arrows of focus

coming out from all sides, it might not look so bad at first glance. But imagine if we combined all those areas into one arrow. Using the same canvas, the arrow would be off the diagram!

As an entrepreneur, focusing all your energy on one thing can significantly improve your odds at being successful. As the saying goes, "the riches are in the niches." Instead of chasing several opportunities at once, focus on one product or service delivery that you can be prolific at. Your time will be better spent, and the financial rewards will be significant. Take, for instance, your primary care doctor. When you visit the doctor, it's typically for a routine appointment such as an annual physical. If the doctor does your readings and notices an abnormal heart pattern, they will likely send you to a heart specialist. The heart specialist will perform their specialized procedures, then send you on your way. According to a recent survey, the average primary care physician makes $261,000 while the heart specialist makes

$427,000—nearly double the salary! [13]Even if you spent the same amount of time with the heart specialist (usually less), the heart specialist gets paid over twice the amount of the primary care physician.

How does this apply to the veteran business owner? Well, let's take a look at the wildly successful founder of Apple. When Steve Jobs returned to the then-near-bankrupt company in 1997 (after being fired several years earlier), Jobs wanted to find out which products to focus on, so he asked his team of top managers, "Which one do I tell my friends to buy?" When he didn't get a

---

[13] https://www.merritthawkins.com/news-and-insights/blog/job-search-advice/physician-starting-salaries-by-specialty-2018-vs-2017/

simple answer, Jobs eliminated nearly 70% of Apple's products. One year later, the almost-bankrupt company turned a very healthy $309 million profit. At the time of this writing, Apple is worth more than $700 billion and growing.

Pareto's Principle, also known as the 80/20 rule, states that in most cases roughly 80% of the effects come from 20% of the causes. By focusing on one task, one idea, one Prolific Purpose, or business goal at a time, you can significantly increase the odds of business success. Going back to our example of Apple, Apple's mission statement is "bringing the best user experience to its customers through its innovative hardware, software, and services." [14]By intensely focusing on a few products, such as the iPhone—which, as of this writing, accounts for over 60% of Apple's profits—Apple is able to fulfill its Prolific Purpose and achieve Prolific Profit.

Reflections & Actions

1. What are your top five distractions?

_____

2. What are you going to do to eliminate those distractions?

_____

3. What's ONE thing you need to start focusing on in your business?

_____

---

[14] https://fourweekmba.com/apple-mission-statement-vision-statement/

CHAPTER 6

Mapping Out Your Domination

As an entrepreneur, you must focus on the one thing that can significantly improve your odds at being successful in business. As we discussed in the previous chapter, instead of chasing several opportunities at once, focus on one product or service delivery where you can be prolific. When I think about the importance of focus and goal setting, I often think of the metaphor of driving. Let's assume that you are going on a long road trip, but you don't have GPS or a navigation app to get to your destination. What do you think the chances are that you would arrive somewhere other than you attended? For example, let's say that you were trying to drive from Miami to Toronto. If you forget to put in the directions, you could very quickly end up in New York, Oregon, or somewhere else entirely. Without setting a proper destination, and mapping the route to get there, you will be unaware of the steps to get to your destination. This is why we set goals.

Your Prolific Purpose is the driving force behind going to that destination in the first place. In the road trip example, a Prolific Purpose for taking a road trip might be to spend quality time with your significant other. For the entrepreneur with eight million other tasks, setting goals like this may seem

trivial and like a waste of time—but studies show that written goals can significantly increase your chances of achieving what you want.

A 1979 study performed by Harvard Business School asked a graduating class, "Have you set written goals and created a plan for their attainment?"[15]

Before graduation, they found that:

- 84% of the entire class had set no goals at all
- 13% of the class had set written goals but had no concrete plans
- 3% of the class had both written goals and specific plans

So what were the results? Ten years later, the 13% of the class that had set written goals but had not created plans were making twice as much money as the 84% of the class that had set no goals at all. However, the kicker is that 3% of the class that had both written goals and a plan were making ten times as much as the rest of the 97% of the class!

Endgame

By starting with the end game, you can quickly see how much easier it is to arrive at your destination. You may not necessarily know the step-by-step— or, in our example with the GPS, the turn-by-turn—but if you take consistent action toward your destination, you will significantly increase the chances of achieving your goals. Now that you understand the importance of starting with the end, take a few moments and answer the following:

1. When do you plan on retiring?

2. How much money do you want to have when you retire?

3. Where do you want to live when you retire?

4. At retirement age, what do you want to be doing each day?

---

[15] https://www.wanderlustworker.com/the-harvard-mba-business-school-study-on-goal-setting/

5. What do you want to be your biggest achievement by the time you hit retirement?

Mapping Out Your Future

Now that you've identified how much money you plan to have when you retire, the net worth that you want to achieve, and what you want your life to look like, you now need to start gaining small wins to obtain your big goals.

However, first, let's get clear on where you are. Take a few moments and answer the following questions below.

1. What is your current monthly income?

_____

2. What is your current debt outstanding?

_____

3. What is your current cash in the bank?

_____

4. What is your income goal in 12 months?

_____

5. What is your cash-in-bank goal in 12 months?

_____

Future State: Personal Goals Setting (these don't have to be financial)

Goal 1:

_____

Goal 2:

_____

Goal 3:

_____

Goal 4:

_____

Goal 5:

_____

Goal 6:

_____

Goal 8:

_____

Goal 9:

_____

Goal 10:

_____

Business Goal Setting

One of my favorite quotes comes from the Renaissance artist Michelangelo, who said, "The greater danger for most of us lies not in setting our aim too high and falling short, but in setting our aim too low and achieving our mark." As you go through these questions, I do not want you to hold back. If something pops into your head for what you want to achieve in your business, write it down! Don't overthink it and worry about how to make them happen now. Someone first imagined every creation in this world. Albert Einstein said: "Imagination is more important than knowledge. For knowledge is limited to all we know and understand, while imagination embraces the entire world, and all there will ever be to know and understand."

When it comes to setting goals for your business, you need to have a voice in the back of your head telling you that anything is possible. Let your imagination run wild. If you can imagine it, it can be done.

Goal 1:

_____

Goal 2:

_____

Goal 3:

_____

Goal 4:

_____

Goal 5:

_____

Goal 6:

_____

Goal 7:

_____

Goal 8:

_____

Goal 9:

_____

Goal 10:

_____

10X Goal Setting

One of my favorite business books is the *10X Rule* by Grant Cardone. In his book, Cardone shares that in order to take the level of action that guarantees extraordinary results, you must 10X your goals. This concept goes against most ways of thinking because people believe that if you set your goals too high, you may be demotivated if you don't achieve them. The 10X rule takes the opposite approach and says the only way you can achieve the results you want in life is to 10X your goals. Why? Because we tend to underestimate how much we can do. By taking MASSIVE ACTION on these new 10Xed goals, you will not only achieve your original goals but significantly exceed them.

With this information, let's take a moment and see what your business currently looks like and what it can look like if you 10X your goals.

Metrics	Today	10X
Sales		
Profit		
Employees		
Clients		
Cash		

Now that they are written down, the chance of you acting on your goals significantly increases. When you begin to put your energy and focus towards a goal, there is a very high likelihood that you will come close and, at times, even hit your desired goal. So what does this mean for you and your life? What does this mean for the people (friends, family, coworkers, etc.) around you?

Massive Action

Once you've identified your goals, the next step is to take massive action toward them. On top of setting clear and measurable goals, you need to make an immediate massive action step. Often times when we set goals, we do not end up achieving these goals because we haven't taken any massive action step to force us in the direction of achieving that goal. For example, if you're looking to lose weight, a massive action step is not just saying: "I'm going to

lose weight!" A massive action step would be going into the gym, signing up for a membership, and scheduling a personal training session for the following day. This is considered a massive action step because it puts you in the position to achieve that goal. Ask yourself, "What's the ONE thing I can do that will make everything else either easier or unnecessary?" Here is a 3-part breakdown of this question to unpack the significance of each component:

1.   What's the ONE thing I can do... This part has to do with the action you "can" take, instead of the ONE thing you "should," "could," or "would" do. The word "can" implies action, while the others imply intention.

2.   ... such that by doing it... This part is about specificity. It means that you're about to take a purpose-drive action.

3.   ... everything else will be easier or unnecessary. This final part is about leverage. It says that when you do this ONE thing, everything else you could do to accomplish your goal will now require less effort (or no longer be necessary). For example: hiring a virtual assistant to respond to your emails is a leveraged action that frees up your time. As a result, it makes it easier for you to focus on growing your business.

Success is not a byproduct of fate, luck, or chance. To achieve real success, you must have a burning desire to reach your goals. People who act are the ones who make the most mistakes and learn from them—and only those who act can win in the game of business. You must be willing to accept that failure is part of the path to wealth. As you go out and pursue these goals, you must commit to doing everything in your ability to achieve them.

Even if you don't reach your goal the first time around, you should not view this as a negative thing. One of the drawbacks to our educational system is that perfection is rewarded, and failure is looked down upon. The exciting thing about life is that these rules are somewhat reversed. Though not achieving the goal may seem like a failure, you cannot get to the reward without being willing to fail. You must be willing to put yourself at risk to pursue your goal. It would help if you created goals that stretch you and take massive action to achieve them.

Visualization

One of the most powerful tools to ingrain goals into your mind is through visualization and affirmations. As I mentioned before, everything around you was first created in the mind. The chair that you're sitting in as you read (or listen to) this book, or the clothes that you're wearing, or the house or vehicle that you're in—all of it was created in someone's mind. We often take our minds for granted because they were given to us for free, and like most things in life, we do not value what we get for free. What's so special about your mind is that it is free of physical limits.

Think about it for a second; you can only lift so much weight, you can only run so fast, and you can only jump so high. However, the mind has no limits to what it can imagine and think of. The only limits that you have on the mind are the ones you place on yourself, which is why visualization is such a powerful tool. One of the most amazing tools that come preprogrammed in our minds is our RAS, or the reticular activating system. The RAS is designed to filter out information that you believe is important. For example, your brain is being stimulated with millions of sensory inputs coming in from your environment—colors, sounds, smells, motion—but your mind can only process so much information at one time. Therefore, it uses the RAS to solely focus on the things that you have consciously (or unconsciously) deemed important.

Think about when you first got your car. You may not have noticed that make and model before you purchased it, but afterward, you may have started seeing it everywhere. You can use the same tool to achieve your goals. I recommend starting your day with a visualization exercise. All you need is a few minutes.

Start by closing your eyes and imagining the future you would like to create for yourself. Be very detailed about how this future will look. Where are you going to be? What does the surrounding area look like? How do you feel? What are you wearing? Imagine all these little details and see them in your mind's eye. This may seem "airy-fairy," but many of your favorite celebrities like Arnold Schwarzenegger, Jim Carrey, Conor McGregor, Oprah Winfrey, Sir Richard Branson, Will Smith, Jay-Z, and Denzel Washington have all said that they've used the power of visualization to achieve their goals.

One of the most effective ways to do this is through a vision board. A vision board is a tool used to help clarify, concentrate, and maintain focus on a specific life goal. A vision board is a place to display images that represent whatever you want to be, do, or have in your life. It is an opportunity to create a sacred space that shows what you wish to bring into your life. What you focus on tends to expand and come into existence. When you create a vision board and place it in a space where you see it often, you will find yourself doing short visualization exercises throughout the day.

Head over to ProlificProfit.com to download the Vision Board Template and start putting together pictures of your goals.

Reflections & Actions

1. What's one massive action step you can take based on the information from this book?

_____

CHAPTER 7

Overcoming Your Business Boogeyman

———————○———————

O ne of the critical success factors among successful millionaires and billionaires is that they are able to control their mindsets. The level of success we achieve is significantly impacted by what is happening inside of our minds. On your journey to Prolific Profit, your biggest enemy is not going to be Uncle Sam (though we will talk about how to tackle him later on in this book), it will be overcoming the boogeyman in your mind. This should be empowering because you have 100% control over it (or at least 100% control over your conscious mind). The first step is to recognize what you are choosing to feed your mind and how it is playing into your daily life.

These are what I call your Belief System, which is composed of both Limiting and Prolific Beliefs. According to the National Science Foundation, the average person has about 12,000 to 60,000 thoughts per day[16]. Of those, 80% are negative and 95% are repetitive. These negatives thoughts have several sources, but the main thing to keep in mind is that they all originate from the past. The sad part about it is that we let these negative experiences, lessons, or assumptions from the past dictate our present thinking, which ultimately impacts our future.

Chances are you have several limiting beliefs that you acquired in your childhood—either through your parents or your surroundings—that have

---

[16] https://tlexinstitute.com/how-to-effortlessly-have-more-positive-thoughts/

prevented you from achieving the financial success you deserve. These limiting beliefs constrain us from acting and achieving our goals.

Overcoming Your Limiting Beliefs

Now that we have discussed and explored limiting beliefs, it's now time to discuss how to plant Prolific Beliefs. Contrary to popular belief, successful business owners are not inherently lucky, nor do they possess any real advantage over the average person. The one thing that separates the Prolific from the Non-Prolific, however, is their mindset. According to Paul Koeck, MD, "hyperactive negative thoughts are developed in your right prefrontal cortex. In the right front part of your brain, just above your eyeball, you will find your right prefrontal cortex (PFC). This is the part of the brain which is responsible for your negative thoughts." [17]Therefore, by gaining control over our limiting beliefs, we then have the ability to influence our PFC.

Just as limiting beliefs prevent you from achieving success, Prolific Beliefs can put you in the fast lane to achieving financial success. Just take a look at some of the most financially successful people in the world. If you begin to study their career, listen to their interviews, or receive any mentorship from them, you will find that they all share a particular set of beliefs. They may have a unique style and approach to achieving financial success, but what they have in common is that they do not allow negativity or limiting beliefs to occupy much of their time.

---

[17] https://www.ncbi.nlm.nih.gov/pmc/articles/PMC2907136/

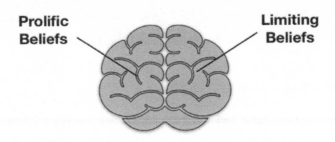

Prolific Beliefs **Limiting Beliefs**

Here are some common Limiting Beliefs and Prolific Beliefs:

Limiting Belief	Prolific Belief
Financial scarcity	Financial abundance
Not worthy of great wealth	Deserve to be rich
Money is about status	Money is about freedom
Focus on cost	Focus on value
Give with an expectation to receive	Give freely without any expectations
The more money you make, the more problems you have	The more money you make, the fewer problems you will have
Getting rich is outside your control	Getting rich is an inside job
Financial abundance is nice to have	Financial abundance is my duty

The great news is that we have the ability to change this thinking simply by changing our word choice. Let's start unraveling these limiting beliefs through an exercise I like to call "Destroying Your Limiting Beliefs."

Destroying Your Limiting Beliefs

Step 1: Write out a goal you identified in the previous section

_____

Step 2: Write out two reasons why you cannot accomplish this goal

_____

Reason 1- Why this is hard:

_____

Reason 2 - Why this is hard:

_____

Step 3: Now take the words in Step 2 and rewrite the sentences in a positive light, explaining why you CAN hit the goal you have set out for yourself

_____

Write out two reasons why you can accomplish this goal. Reason 1 - Why I can do it:

_____

Reason 2 - Why I can do it:

_____

Empowering, isn't it? Go back to Step 3 and re-read the reasons why you CAN accomplish the goal you set for yourself. Then go back and repeat the exercise for all the other goals you listed in the previous section.

The problem with our minds is that we are very negative towards the things we want to accomplish. This may come from either outside sources or internal thoughts telling you, "NO, you cannot do that," or "NO, you cannot hit that goal." Master this, and you will have complete mastery over your future.

Affirmations

Along with visualization, affirmations can be a potent tool to help you achieve your goals. Your Prolific Purpose is a form of affirmation because you are affirming what is driving you to achieve your goals.

Affirmations are a great way to counter any limiting beliefs that you hold. The framework to develop an affirmation is simple.

1. A good affirmation should be in the present tense and therefore should start with the words "I am," because the future begins today.

2. You want to make your affirmation short enough so you can commit it to memory and say it daily.

3. Don't place any limits on it. For example, you can say, "I am creative, powerful, energetic, and producing at least $1,000,000 a month for my business."

By making an affirmation limitless, this opens the possibility of what you can achieve and helps bring the future to the present. By making statements about the future in the present tense, our brains will focus our attention on actions that we can take. Why? Because it craves congruency, and with that congruency, we will develop the feelings associated with achieving this affirmation. We've all experienced this exact same process with fear. Fear is nothing but an emotional response induced by a perceived threat (in the future), which causes a change in brain and organ function, which in turn can change our behavior. Just as fear can negatively influence your behavior, self-affirmations can positively influence your behavior and bring you closer to the future you desire.

Reflections & Actions

1. What are some of your limiting beliefs?

_____

2. How can you turn those limiting beliefs into Prolific Beliefs?

_____

3. What are your three favorite affirmations?

_____

PART II

POWER

CHAPTER 8

Parlez-Vous Business?
The Language Of Business

L ike most of you, when I go to a networking event, one of the first questions I get asked is, "What do you do?" At that moment, I know one of two things is going to happen when I say I'm an accountant. I will either get an inauthentic "Oh wow! That's nice..." followed by a quick getaway to the "bathroom," or I get hit with a million questions for free advice. If this awkward exchange doesn't result in one of those two outcomes, a kind soul may ask: "What made you get into that?"

When I search deep within my memory bank to remember why I was willing to sit through several thousand hours learning about numbers, debits and credits, cash and accrual accounting, and other forms of what may seem like educational torture, I think back to the time when my college economics professor shared that "accounting is the language of business." At that time, I knew I wanted to be an entrepreneur, knew I wanted to be wealthy, and I knew that I wanted to live life on my own terms. When I heard this statement, I immediately knew that accounting was the path to achieving these goals.

While part of this belief was true, knowing accounting did not make me rich all on its own. However, knowing accounting did enable me to unlock the language of building a Prolific business. A lack of understanding of core accounting principles will impact a business's ability to grow profits or sustain financial success. Therefore, to truly be successful in business, you must have a general understanding of accounting. It is not enough to pay your accountant to take your transactions and financial activities and have them throw those numbers on financial statements. If you're lucky, you may have an accountant who is willing to walk you through precisely what those numbers mean, but at the end of the day, it is your responsibility as a business owner to truly understand those numbers. You can't be effective at the game of business if you don't understand the language of business.

It is useless to know that your body temperature is 98.6 Fahrenheit if you don't know how that number is derived or what to compare it to. Without context, that number is like a foreign language. Likewise, as a business owner, you must use your understanding of the language of business to drive your business activities. In short, you want to be able to compare trends over time and measure the relationships between numbers within a given period.

In this section, I will try to give you a crash course in the world of accounting without boring your eyes out. If you've been in business for even a short period, you are probably aware of the different financial statements. The three main financial statements you need to be mindful of are: the Balance Sheet, Income Statement, and Cash Flow Statement. (The fourth is the Statement of Owner's Equity which we will not get into in this book.) Keith Cunningham—

internationally known speaker, business guru, and acclaimed author— states that "only 50% of business owners get financial statements, and only 3% know how to read them."[18] This is a very telling statistic and explains a lot about why so many businesses fail. If a business owner does review their financials, they place an overwhelming amount of focus on the profit. While profit is important (and we'll discuss in-depth how to maximize this number), we need to be keenly aware of the other factors that impact your business

---

[18] https://www.tonyrobbins.com/business/reading-financial-statements/

and how profit even came to be in the first place. This leads me to the discussion of the first financial statement, the Balance Sheet.

The Balance Sheet: One Man's Trash is Another Man's Treasure

Just as the name implies, the balance sheet is a financial statement that must balance. One the left side of the balance sheet, you have your assets. By definition, an asset is a useful or valuable thing, person, or quality. For simplicity, let's call assets the "things" you own. The things you can have in your business are Cash, Accounts Receivable, Inventory, Property, Plants, and Equipment (PPE). Cash is the money that you can spend in your business; Accounts Receivable, on the other hand, is money that is *owed* to you by your customer. This is not cash, but a promise to pay you for a current or future product or service. Inventory are things you purchased that you intend to resell. If you are a service business, chances are you have very few things that are considered inventory. Here are a few more examples of business assets:

- Investments
- Land
- Buildings
- Equipment
- Trademarks/Patents/Other
- Intangible Assets (i.e., reputation or goodwill)

So that's the left side of the balance sheet. On the right side, we find the things you owe to someone else, also called liabilities. By definition, a liability is a thing for which someone is responsible, especially a debt or financial obligation. Things you owe in the business world are categorized by Accounts Payable, Notes Payable, or Taxes Payable. Accounts Payable is what you owe your vendors and suppliers. Notes Payable is what you owe a lender such as a financial institution. Taxes Payable are (unfortunately) the money you owe the government. Here are a few more examples of business liabilities:

- Loans payable
- Bonds payable
- Interest payable
- Wages payable
- Customer deposits
- Deferred revenue

The difference between what you own and what you owe is called "equity". If you are a homeowner, you may be familiar with this term, as it represents the current value of your home (asset) minus the mortgage (liability). In the business world, you can also acquire equity through shareholders, investors,

other business owners (shareholder's equity), and the profits you've made in the past that you kept in the business (retained earnings).

One thing that has always fascinated me about the balance sheet is that it made me realize that someone's asset can be another person's liability. The home you currently own is the bank's asset, but it is your liability until you can sell it for above the amount you owe or pay off the note.

You'll often hear the balance sheet called a "point-in-time" financial statement because it records your business transactions up to that point. You'll notice that your balance sheets will say "As of"; it shows where each of those "things" stands at that point in time.

Balance Sheet	
Things = Assets Cash Accounts Receivable Inventory PPE	**Owe = Liabilities** Accounts Payable Taxes Payable Notes Payable
	Own = Equity Owner Investment Earnings - Current Earnings - Retained

The Income Statement: It's A-ccrual World

The trickiest and most notoriously deceitful financial statement is the Income Statement. For starters, the financial statement is given many names such as the "P&L," "profit and loss statement," or, less commonly, "statement of

operations". Don't get hung up on the differences in the wording, which is more of a "tomayto, tomahto" deal. The important thing to know is that the income statement records your sales (or revenue) and expenses (or costs). Simple enough, right? Not quite. What makes this statement tricky is the concept of cash-basis vs. accrual-method accounting. Cash-basis accounting records transactions based on the actual cash flow in your business. For instance, in cash-basis accounting you can only record a sale when you receive cash for that sale. If you invoice a client, the accrual method of accounting allows you to record that as a sale, while in cash-basis accounting this transaction is disregarded until the cash from the customer is received. The same goes for expenses; the expense is only recorded when the actual outlay of cash occurs. In the United States, the accrual basis of accounting for tax purposes became an option in 1916.

For the sake of consistency, the sales produced in the period are "matched" to the costs "incurred" during that period. Revenues can come in all shapes and forms, like "Operating Revenues" or "Non-Operating Revenue" (such as revenue made from the interest of an asset you own) or "Gains on the Sale of Assets." For expenses, you have items like "Cost of Goods Sold," "Depreciation," "Losses," and other costs you would expect from a business. Expenses such as depreciation, losses, and cost of goods sold are non-cash expenses, meaning that the cash outflow does not match the actual cash exchange—this is part of the reason why the income statement doesn't reflect real cash made in a business. Accrual accounting gives you an overall understanding of your financial performance based on matching the revenue earned with the expenses incurred, regardless of when you collected the revenue or paid the expenses.

The income statement is represented over some time (months, quarters, or years). If your revenue exceeds costs, then you have a profit. However, due to the nature of the accrual accounting method, showing a profit doesn't necessarily mean you have cash. This is why many business owners think their business is "profitable" based on the numbers on the income statement but feel broke at the end of each period.

Income Statement
Revenue (Sales)
Expenses
Profit

The Statement of Cash Flows: "Cash Flow" is King

The third and final financial statement is the "Cash Flow Statement". Believe it or not, there are several forms of cash. I don't mean currencies or different dead presidents. I mean that the origin and role of cash that you receive in your business can be broken up into three main categories: "operating cash," "investing cash," and "financing cash". Operating cash is the cash you receive

from generating a sale or collecting money that a customer owes to you (i.e., Accounts Receivable). This cash can be used for several different purposes, but for now, suffice to say that this cash can be used to pay expenses or pay back your vendors/suppliers (i.e., Accounts Payable).

Investing cash is the cash you receive from selling assets that are not necessarily sold as part of your day-to-day business. These assets could be a piece of property you own, such as land or equipment (i.e., machinery). It's called "investing" because it's an asset you've invested in for your business and you happen to sell it.

Lastly, financing cash is cash you receive from borrowing money from a financial institution, such as a bank, or raising money from investors. This type of cash typically needs to be paid back and, therefore, can potentially limit your ability to generate this cash flow again.

Statement of Cash Flows	
Beginning Cash	x
Operating Cash Flow	+ / -
Investing Cash Flow	+ / -
Financing Cash Flow	+ / -
Ending Cash	y

The Bottom Line

As you can see, your financials are a useful tool to assess the health of your business. Each financial statement has a different purpose and provides different insights into how well you're able to generate profit, build equity, and manage cash flow. While we just scratched the surface on these topics, this will give you a good sense of how each transaction flows into financial statements. As you will discover, by developing a better understanding of accounting, you'll be better equipped to develop better business practices to improve these numbers.

Reflections & Actions

1. What financial statement have you focused on the most?

   _____

2. What financial statement have you focused on the least?

   _____

Go to ProlificProfit.com to download your free full-page colored infographic of the Language of Business.

CHAPTER 9

Your Books = Your Story

———————o———————

I f I haven't lost you with all the accounting stuff, you'll notice that the financial statements tell a particular story about your business. As a business owner, you need to be able to read and understand your story to tell what's going on. Just like any good story (or middle school essay), there is an introduction, a body, and a conclusion. To keep things simple, take the well-known nursery rhyme of Jack and Jill.

Jack and Jill Went up the hill
To fetch a pail of water Jack fell down
And broke his crown,
And Jill came tumbling after.

Balance Sheet (Introduction/Conclusion): As I mentioned previously, the Balance Sheet is a snapshot of what is going on in your business. The assets, liabilities, and equity in your business are displayed at a specific moment in time. The balance is like both the introduction *and* conclusion of your business' story. It is a snapshot of where the business was at a point in time.

For instance, if you started your business at the beginning of this year, looking at the balance sheet at that point in time will show what assets, liabilities, and equity the business had at the outset. At the end of the year, your balance sheet will likely show different balances, showing what you had after that first year. Using the nursery rhyme of Jack and Jill, the balance sheet as of

January 20XX would be "Jack and Jill," the December 20XX would be "And Jill came tumbling after."

Income Statement (Body): These statements are the story that is told between the balance sheet. It shows what happened to your business over a period of time. The income statement is presented as "for," like "for 1/1/20-12/31/20." Alternatively, if you find yourself asking, "How did I increase my earnings?" the income statement will tell that story. The "net income," which is income minus expenses from your income statement, gets reported on your balance sheet in the "current earnings" section. Going back to our nursery rhyme example, this would be "Went up the hill, to fetch a pail of water, Jack fell down, and broke his crown."

Statement of Cash Flow (Characters, Setting, Plot): If you're wondering, "How the heck did my cash go down?" look no further than the cash flow statement. You also have a section on the balance sheet called "retained earnings," which is the cumulative balance of all the earnings you received "as of" the balance sheet date. The "ending cash" that is reported on the cash flow statement also moves to the balance, but this time gets placed in the "cash" section under assets. The statement of cash flows takes one asset—cash—and categorizes it in three different buckets. This metaphor may be a stretch, but I would compare it to the elements of a story (characters, setting, plot). The story is asset (cash) and the elements are the different components that make up the story (operating, investing, financing).

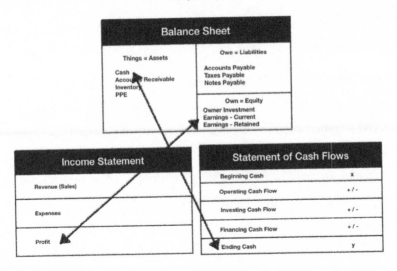

The Plot Twist

If this is new information for you, your next response should naturally be, "Wait a minute, if cash and earnings (profits) go on two separate sections in the balance sheet, then..." YES! Accounting profits do not equal cash. You can't pay your bills, give yourself a salary, take a fancy vacation with profits. Try paying your dinner bill with your "profits". If they don't put you in the crazy house or arrest you, you will need to find some cash...FAST.

This simple yet profound concept can dramatically change how you operate your business. According to a U.S. Bank study, 82% of business failures are due to poor cash flow management, or a poor understanding of how cash flow contributes to the business. You may be wondering, "If cash flow is so hard to come by, why did you call this book Prolific Profit?" Besides the fact that it makes for an impressive book title and branding, there are several reasons why profit matters. But before we get into that, I first want to explain the alchemy of business.

Reflections & Actions

1. What problems do you have when reviewing your financial statements?

_____

2. How often do you review your financial statements?

_____

CHAPTER 10

Converting Nothing To Something

A lchemy is an ancient practice famously known for turning lead into gold. The practitioner of this act is called an alchemist, and as a business owner, you are the modern-day alchemist turning what's in your business ("things" or assets) into gold ("cash"). Therefore, as a business owner, your "one job" is to convert assets to cash. Your ability to perform this transmutation determines whether you are at the top of the Hierarchy of Business Success or at the bottom.

What should be most relevant to business owners (and investors) is the following:

- Effectiveness: Doing the right things for the business (acquiring and converting assets to revenues).
- Efficiency: Doing things right (converting revenues to profit).
- Productivity: Output and input (converting profits to cash).

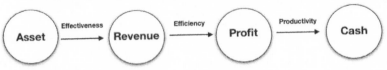

Accounting is full of ratios (which I painfully had to commit to memory for the CPA exam) that tell you how a business is doing based on the figures of the financial statement. There are several formulas that can paint that picture, but for now, let's focus on the ones that measure effectiveness, efficiency, and productivity.

Effectiveness Ratio

To be effective in your business, you must be able to convert your assets into revenues. Assets, as we discussed, are presented on the balance sheet, while revenue is presented on the income statement. One thing to note is that there are also assets that are not reported on the balance sheet, such as employees. To calculate your effectiveness ratio, also known as Asset Turnover, divide your revenue by assets.

By effectively utilizing these resources, you can increase your effectiveness. For example, if you increased revenues by 30% and increased assets by 5%, this ratio will show you that you've increased your effectiveness by 6X. The higher you increase this ratio, the better.

$$\frac{\textbf{Revenue}}{\textbf{Assets}} = \textbf{Effectiveness \%}$$

Efficiency Ratio

Efficiency measures how well you are converting revenue to profit while incurring the least amount of expenses as possible. To calculate this ratio, also known as profit margin, divide your profits by revenues. This is another

number that you want to keep as high as possible. For example, if you increased profits by 50% by lowering expenses and also increased revenue by 10% by increasing prices, you will see a 5X boost in your efficiency ratio.

$$\frac{\textbf{Profits}}{\textbf{Revenue}} = \textbf{Efficiency \%}$$

Profitability Ratio

If we combined the effectiveness and efficiency ratios, we would get a profitability ratio, also known as "Return on Assets" (ROA). The higher the ratio is, the better you are at effectively managing assets to produce greater amounts of net income. A positive ROA ratio usually indicates an upward profit trend as well.

$$\frac{\textbf{Effectiveness}}{\textbf{Efficiency}} = \textbf{Return on Assets}$$

or

$$\frac{\textbf{Revenue}}{\textbf{Assets}} \quad \textbf{x} \quad \frac{\textbf{Profits}}{\textbf{Revenue}} = \frac{\textbf{Profits}}{\textbf{Assets}}$$

Productivity Ratio

The final part of our alchemy from turning assets to cash is the productivity ratio. As I mentioned before, the cash has three different forms. As business owners, our focus should be on operating cash flow. Therefore, the productivity ratio, also known as the operating cash flow ratio, is calculated by dividing operating cash flow by profits.

$$\frac{\textbf{Operating Cash Flow}}{\textbf{Profits}} = \textbf{Operating Cash Flow Ratio}$$

Just like the previously mentioned ratios, you want this ratio to be increasing period over period. What happens if we combine all three ratios to see how effective your efficiency is at making your assets productive (i.e., convert to cash)?

$$\textbf{Effectiveness x Efficiency x Productivity} = \frac{\textbf{Operating Cash Flow}}{\textbf{Assets}}$$

You Had One Job: What Business Owners Must Be Laser-Focused On

Among my favorite online memes (those funny images using a bit of text) is the "You Had One Job" meme that originated from a clip in the film *Ocean's*

Eleven. In this particular clip, Basher Tarr (Don Cheadle) enters a vault his team was supposed to disarm. After he enters, the alert goes off, which ruins the heist. Basher Tarr reacts, "Oh, leave it all out! You tossers! You had ONE job." This one clip has led to thousands of memes showcasing instances where people completely screw up on the job.

As a business owner, your ONE job is to maximize the operating cash flow your business generates with the minimum amount of assets. Yes, you must be a good leader. Yes, you must provide excellent service to your customer. Yes, there are a million things you must do as a business owner—but the bottom-line activity that you *must* do if you want to achieve the highest level of the Hierarchy of Business Success is to improve these ratios effectively.

There are several things you can do in your business to improve these ratios, but at the end of the day, these ratios should be an indicator of how your business is doing.

Taking a look at the formula can show you how you can screw this up. Allowing assets to go up and operating cash flow to go down can negatively impact your chances of doing your one job well. Since the bottom line of both your stories (remember, the income statement and statement of cash flows) is profit and cash, let's spend some time discussing how to maximize these numbers.

Reflections & Actions

1. What are your prior month and current month ratios?

   _____

2. Why do you feel like they are increasing or decreasing?

   _____

3. What is your one job as a business owner?

   _____

Go to ProlificProfit.com to download your free full-page colored infographic of the Alchemy of Business.

CHAPTER 11

How To Avoid Bankruptcy

I haven't spoken much about bankruptcy in this book, but given we're at Chapter 11, I think it's fitting we get the conversation going. If you're not aware, Chapter 11 is a chapter of Title 11, the United States Bankruptcy Code, which permits reorganization under the bankruptcy laws of the United States.

According to the American Bankruptcy Institute (ABI), over 23,000 businesses filed for bankruptcy in 2017.

One of the first steps you can take to reduce the risk of this happening is to achieve Prolific Profit, which, as we discussed, is recorded in the income statement. Therefore, the only two options you have to improve profitability is to:

1. Increase revenues
2. Decrease expenses

Like most things in life, the concept is simple, but the application is not easy— which is why we need a whole book to explain it all. At the beginning of this book, we discussed a lot of mindset and psychology. The reason for this is because, as humans, we are emotional creatures and allow emotions to drive our behavior. In psychology, this is called cognitive bias. Cognitive biases are behaviors that deviate from the expected outcomes of rational judgment. Psychologist and economist Daniel Kahneman was awarded the

2002 Nobel Prize in Economics for his contributions to behavioral economics. In his bestselling book, *Thinking, Fast and Slow*, Kahneman shares the concept of "framing". Framing is the context in which choices are presented. In one of his experiments, subjects were asked whether they would opt for surgery if the "survival" rate was 90 percent, while others were told that the "mortality" rate was 10 percent. [19] The first framing increased acceptance, even though the situation was no different. Instead of trying to fight this cognitive bias, we can use it to our advantage by framing the way we look at profit.

My favorite book on this subject is Mike Michalowicz's *Profit First*. Like Mike (couldn't resist), we both believe that GAAP does not serve entrepreneurs well. While it is essential to have generally accepted accounting principles for consistency and transparency, small business owners (99.7% of businesses[20]) need a system that works for them. By using our cognitive bias to our advantage, Mike cleverly switched the traditional Sales - Expenses = Profits formula to Sales - Profits = Expenses.

This simple yet profound idea not only reframes our focus to profits (in cash terms) but also guarantees profitability. I won't take away too much of his thunder, but here are the CliffsNotes.

- **Step #1**: Set up five bank accounts with your current business checking account.
- **Step #2**: Give each account a different name. Mike recommends the following: Income, Profit, Owner's Comp, Tax, and Operating Expenses.

---

[19] https://www.bloomberg.com/news/articles/2011-10-27/book-review-thinking-fast-and-slow-by-daniel-kahneman
20 https://www.businessinsider.com/why-small-businesses-fail-infographic-2017-8?r=US&IR=T

- **Step #3**: Set up two new savings accounts at different business banks to remove the temptation of "borrowing" from these accounts: Profit Hold and Tax Hold.

I'll let you read his book for all the details, but in short, this system has several benefits. For starters, it takes away our need to force ourselves to be logical. By doing a one-time setup of different bank accounts, it removes the temptation of overspending on expenses or paying ourselves first. Secondly, it puts you as a business owner in the position to become more innovative with your business and identify ways to be more effective, efficient, and productive in your ability to convert assets to cash (your ONE job). In regard to revenue, you need to ask yourself every day:

- What are some cost-effective ways to increase revenue?
- Can I change pricing?
- Can I change the estimation process on client jobs?
- Is there a way to restructure bonuses and incentives for sales team members?
- Is there a way to restructure bonuses and incentives for managers and executives to better drive results?

Another great quote from Mike's book is, "It's smarter to dig a well than make it rain. Focusing solely on increasing sales is like setting up a bunch of rain barrels next to your house and doing some frantic rain dance in a loincloth while ignoring a massive water source beneath your feet." In plain English, you have way more money than you realize. The problem with many business owners is not client acquisition (this has become easier than ever with social media platforms), it's maximizing profits in their business.

Going from Big to Bankrupt: How Not to Grow Your Business

The problem with many business owners is that they try to grow too big too quickly. While this may work in the short-term (during an expanding economy), as economic conditions worsen the business owner finds themselves running out of cash and running from debt collectors.

By definition, there are two ways you can maximize something: you can make it as large as possible or make the best use of it. Successful business owners know that they need to focus on the latter by making the best use of the resources they have. This may not be the sexiest approach, but would you rather be sexy or rich? Would you rather be poor or prolific? The choice is yours.

The fastest path to sustainable Prolific Profit maximization (which means that it is able to be upheld or protected during an economic contraction) is taking care of the low-hanging fruit (which are unnecessary expenses).

As part of your one job to convert assets to cash, expenses will inevitably play a role—but the way you view expenses must change. To successfully transform these assets (cash, inventory, property, and equipment), you must view expenses as an investment. Investment is the action or process of

investing money for profit. The way to test whether something is an investment for your business is whether it's bringing in new money or tapping into old money. If you can't easily correlate how an expense is increasing the number of new customers or serving your existing customer base, then chances are it needs to go.

I know you may be thinking this sounds bean counter-ish (I warned you early on that I possess some of these traits), but the truth of the matter is if you become accustomed to blowing money on unnecessary expenses, you won't have much room to improve revenue when tough economic times hit.

You may be saying to yourself, "Well, I can't possibly eliminate every single expense, can I?" And the short answer is "No," but by first identifying how to eliminate unnecessary expenses or expenses that do not directly bring in more revenue, you optimize your business for growth. Imagine growing and scaling an unnecessarily large expense intensive business. The expenses are like an increasingly large snowball pushed up a mountain. Sooner or later, the snowball will become too big to push and will fall back quickly and violently. This may seem counterintuitive, but if you don't operate your business as efficiently as possible (meaning you make the best use of the assets that you have), more sales can actually make you *less* profitable. A few strategies to consider for reducing expenses are the following:

- Renegotiating merchant processing fees
- Cost remediation process to determine superfluous expenses
- Budgeting and forecasting for improved cash flow
- Cash management and planning
- Analyzing vendors and quotes

There's no point in having a ton of revenue if you continue to overspend. The magic is that by increasing your profit margins, you can improve your company's profits without the need for increased sales. Unfortunately, many business owners think to themselves, "Oh no, sales are down, let's crank up the marketing!" without diagnosing the real problem. It's easy to change your focus on your marketing efforts because you get to do cool things like update your website, create Facebook Ads and experiment with Google Adwords— but while these things may drive more clients to your business, client retention is a much more effective means of converting assets to revenues.

Reflections & Actions

1. How do you plan on setting up your different cash accounts?

    _____

2. What are some unnecessary expenses (other than your lousy accountant) you can eliminate today?

    _____

CHAPTER 12

Sell More, Work Less

A s we mentioned at the end of the previous chapter, the single most powerful solution to effectively and efficiently improve your revenue is not client acquisition (unless you have no clients whatsoever!), but client retention. According to research by Frederick Reichheld of Bain & Company, increasing customer retention rates by 5% increases profits by 25% to 95%.[21]

If your goal as a business owner is to effectively, efficiently, and productively convert assets to cash (which it better be), then you MUST direct your focus on client retention. Think about it: you spend all this time blogging, posting, sharing, promoting, networking, spending, and sometimes begging to get a client or customer. Why is it that so many entrepreneurs spend so little time serving the people who have *already* entrusted their hard-earned money to you?

Part of being Prolific is to have seeds (clients) planted in the ground, but more important than that is to water (continued service) them so you can truly be prolific. It's not only cheaper to service existing clients, but it also saves you time. According to the book *Marketing Metrics*, businesses have a 60 to 70% chance of selling to an existing customer while the probability of selling to a

---

[21] https://www.forbes.com/sites/jiawertz/2018/09/12/dont-spend-5-times-more-attracting-new-customers-nurture-the-existing-ones/#d9defe15a8e0

new prospect is only 5% to 20%. [22] Based on that statistic alone, that's a 14X increase in close rates. How's that for effective and efficient?!?

The reasons should be obvious, and they have a lot to do with another cognitive bias called loss aversion. Loss aversion refers to people's tendency to prefer avoiding losses over acquiring equivalent gains. For example, people have a stronger emotional reaction to losing $5 than finding $5. Once a client has already made the leap with your business, their perception of risk significantly decreases. They've developed a relationship with you (hopefully good) and they know what to expect. Therefore, the most lucrative (but non-reportable) asset you have in your business is customer loyalty. Simon Sinek says that "loyalty is when people are willing to turn down a better product or price to continue doing business with you." Now that's POWER!

Based on my experience with my own business, and from helping countless other business owners increase their profitability, the most effective way to do this is through the value ladder. A value ladder takes the services you are providing and maps them out in a logical order to maximize the long-term value you can provide in products and/or services to your existing customer. In the beginning, you want to keep it simple. You want to listen to your customers because you will uncover the components of your ladder by working with paying clients on an ongoing basis. As you find out more needs from your clients, you can add new steps to your value ladder.

First, you want to start with your core offerings. When you bring a client on board, you have to think about all of the different ways you can help them, both now and in the future. Will they continue to work with you beyond the one service that drew them to you in the first place? It's so much easier to

---

[22] https://www.forbes.com/sites/patrickhull/2013/12/06/tools-for-entrepreneurs-to-retain-clients/#1fef03da2443

build a new business out of your existing clients than it is to go out and find new work. When you create a value ladder, you move your clients through a lifecycle of services, provide them with more value, and get paid more in return.

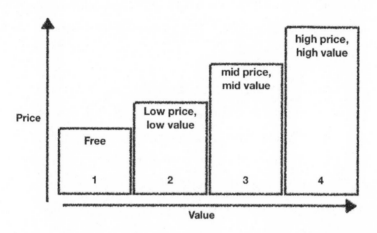

Many of my clients get intimidated by this concept and feel like they're overselling to their client. This couldn't be further from the truth. Take, for instance, this book. Let's say you paid $25 for this book. Do you think it is worth $25? Your initial reaction may be "yes," but that is likely incorrect. The reason you were willing to spend $25 on this book (or anything else) is that you believed one thing: the value of the item you purchased is worth more than the amount (cash) you paid. In other words, you believed what the book can do for your life is worth more than what you paid for it. Therefore, by selling your client more of your products and services, you actually provide

more value. The value you provide to your clients is measured in how much more the same prospect (i.e., a future customer in search of a product or service) pays you than your competition. If your clients are paying you more, you offer more value.

There are several ways to re-engage current and past customers. Here are a few:

1. Show that you care: Keep in touch with clients by sending them a card or email for their birthdays and holidays. You can go a step further and make them a quick video wishing them well and thanking them for patronage.

2. Systemize Outreach: Be sure to track touchpoints with your customers and set reminders to reach out. There are several tools and systems that you can use to reconnect with your customers digitally. You can also provide them with a good piece of free content, like a report or a checklist on a problem that you know they may currently have. Below are some of the most used channels for customer retention:

    - Mobile messaging
    - Email
    - Mobile apps
    - Mobile and web push notification
    - Social media marketing

3. Keep Things Positive: According to Harvard Business Review, 48% of customers who had a negative experience told ten or more others. [23] This not only impacts your ability to resell a current customer but significantly affects your ability to attract new customers. Look for ways to improve your new customer experience to keep them in business.

4. Ask for Referrals: Referral marketing is a close second to upselling existing customers since existing customers can help alleviate the loss aversion. The most effective way to ask for referrals is right after

---

[23] https://hbr.org/2010/07/stop-trying-to-delight-your-customers

providing an exceptional service. If you like, reward the customer through a discount on a future service or a cost-effective freebie.

Reflections & Actions

1. What is your value ladder?

---

2. What actions will you take today to upsell your current clients?

CHAPTER 13

The Big 4: Consistent Cash Flow Is King

A s I've mentioned previously in this book, more than 70 percent of businesses don't make it to year ten. We've identified the culprits and activities that are responsible for this disheartening statistic, but many business owners still believe that luck, passion, drive, work ethic, marketing, and closing sales will keep their doors open. While all of these play an important role as to whether a business will succeed or fail, the bottom line is they ran out of cash.

A business owner can't pay their bills, invest in their business, pay taxes, or reduce debt without cash. Cash flow is king, and when the king dies, there is no queen, prince, or princess that will take its place. Therefore, as a business owner, you must maximize cash flow. As you've learned, not all cash is the same, and of all forms of cash we discussed (operating, investing, and financing), operating cash flow (OCF) reigns supreme.

It's not sustainable to sell equipment or furniture (investing cash flow), nor is it sustainable to borrow money from the banks, friends, or family members (financing cash flow). Instead of focusing on raising cash (which is essentially what ICF and FCF are), you need to become an operating cash flow machine.

The income statement gives us two ways to do this: sell more or spend less. The balance sheet, on the other hand, provides us with three options: reduce accounts receivable days (average days it takes to get money from your customers), reduce inventory days (average days it takes to sell inventory), increase accounts payable (average days it takes to pay your bills).

Easy enough, right? Yes! With a strategic plan and focus on increasing these metrics over time, you can go from a business that is "suffering" to a business that is successful in a shorter window of time. Let's talk about each one of these individually to see what options we have to improve them.

Decrease Accounts Receivable Days

Probably one of the most frustrating things about entrepreneurship is dealing with delayed and uncollectible receivables. The longer you wait, the less oxygen (operating cash) your business has. With some businesses, customers must pay in full at the time of purchase (such as a grocery store), but for many business owners, they must work on lowering the days that accounts receivables are outstanding. Even a reduction of a few days can make a big difference to a struggling business. Business owners have a couple of options when it comes to getting receivables more quickly from their customers.

1. *Early communication:* You need to communicate up front to your customer that you expect prompt payment—in full—for services rendered. Depending on the relationship you have with the customer, you can share with them the impact that late payments has on your business.

2. *Consistent communication:* Most invoicing software has automated reminders before the due date to make your customer aware of an upcoming invoice. For new customers, be sure to verify their billing information to ensure a smooth process. For any customers significantly past due on their bill, confirm receipt of the invoice. If

you know they have received the invoice, make sure to stay on top of them by calling, texting, and emailing, frequently and repeatedly.

3. *Age your accounts receivable:* In addition to the financial ratio metrics previously mentioned, you should also be tracking the following: (a) How many invoices are past due? (b) How many have unapproved discounts? (c) How often does the sales team override standard terms (extending payment agreements past 15 or 30 days)? (d) If overrides are frequent, should you change your terms? You should create what is called an "accounts receivable aging schedule" that shows how long your accounts receivable have not been paid. The longer they haven't been paid, the higher your risk of falling down a level on the Business Success Hierarchy.

4. *Hire a factoring company:* If you're not aware, factoring is when a business sells its receivables to a third-party company known as a "factor". The factor advances (typically 70% to 85%) of the receivable to the business owner, then collects payment on those invoices from the business' customers. The biggest downside is the fee associated with the service, which ranges from 1.15% to 4.5% per 30 days. I would use this as a last resort, but it may be a viable option depending on your business.

Decrease Inventory Days

Sitting inventory can be just as lethal to your operating cash as slow-paying customers. Here are a couple of tips to decrease the number of days you keep inventory sitting around.

1. *Eliminate obsolete inventory.* If it's not selling, it needs to go; it's as simple as that. Obsolete inventory is taking up space on shelves, which you can use for better-selling products.

2. *Just-in-time (JIT) inventory.* Instead of allowing the supplier to dictate how much and when they will send their inventory, analyze your business needs and order inventory only when you need it. To do this effectively, you must understand the demands of your product and forecast any changes in demand.

3. *Shrink shrinkage.* Shrinkage is the reduction of inventory due to wastage or theft. For wastage, this can be improved by implementing JIT. As far as theft, don't dismiss it as a "cost of business"; instead, try to find cost-effective ways to reduce it.

Increase Accounts Payable

Remember, your accounts payable is another business owner's accounts receivable. It's terrible business practice and bad karma to be late on your bills. That being said, if your supplier allows the flexibility (and many will), I believe it's appropriate to negotiate with your supplier to extend the days you have to pay your payables. By being able to pay later, you free up cash flow and allow yourself to put that cash into more productive activities. Here are some steps to increase payables.

- Review your payment agreement and determine the latest day you can pay your bill before incurring a penalty.
- Reach out to your supplier and determine whether you can negotiate longer terms
- Once negotiated terms are set, pay bills on time but not before the agreed-upon date.
- Avoid late charges at all costs. It's just an unnecessary cost and hurts profitability.

To sum up, to ensure that operating cash flow maintains its throne as king in your business, here are the four cash flow laws to abide by:

1. Operating cash flow should be positive

2. Operating cash flow should be higher than profits

3. Operating cash flow should be growing faster than profits

4. Operating cash flow should be bigger than investing cash needs

As amazing as operating cash flow is, believe or not, there is something even more attractive that doesn't get talked enough about in the small business community. It's called free cash flow (FCF). Despite the name, it's not free cash (even though that would be even more amazing!)—instead, free cash flow is the excess balance of cash after investing cash needs are addressed. FCF is a way of looking at a company's cash to determine what's available for distribution among all of the owners. If operating cash flow is king, then free cash flow is the emperor of business. Some would say that FCF is the "fourth bottom line." I say it's the path to Prolific.

FCF is important to investors and creditors because it provides greater assurance that cash will be available for distributions or debt payments. FCF is used accordingly: (1) reinvest in the business (i.e., buy more assets); (2) repay debt; (3) provide distributions to owners or additional compensation.

Here is the final form of the alchemical formula of business.

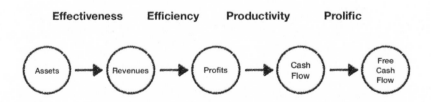

Reflections & Actions

1. How much cash is slipping through your business?

_____

2. On a scale from one to ten, how well are you abiding by the four cash flow laws?

_____

CHAPTER 14

Strategies To Taming The Tax Troll

———————o———————

I want you to take a moment and write down your biggest expenses, either business or personal. When I ask this question on stage, most people in the audience respond with "marketing," "children," "mortgage," "car insurance," or "student loans." While all of these are big expenses, would you agree that if you don't know what your single biggest expense is, you also wouldn't know how to reduce it?

As you probably guessed (considering the name of the chapter), your single biggest expenses are taxes. You may be thinking to yourself, "Well, not for me, I'm in the 22 percent tax bracket, so…" But that's what the government wants you to think! They tax you when you earn money (income tax), they tax you when you buy something (sales tax, and from the same money you got taxed on no less), they tax you on the property you acquire (property tax) and tax you again if you sell it for more than you bought it for (capital gains tax), and unfortunately when you die you get hit with another tax (estate tax). In the end, the average working American pays over 50 percent in taxes.

In your pursuit of Prolific Profit, I believe it's important for you to learn about and tame the beast that is tax. I've found that many business owners also place all the burden and understanding of taxes on their accountant. While it may be painful, business owners need to have a high-level understanding of the tax code given that taxes will (likely) be your single biggest expense. I've helped countless businesses save $10,000 to $100,000 by applying some of the same principles I will share in this section, so pay close attention. Those who don't will pay the biggest expense of all, which is the ignorance tax. The ignorance tax is not directly written in the IRS code, but is a tax you pay nonetheless by:

1. Failing to abide by the IRS rules resulting in fines and penalties
2. Overpaying in taxes due to lack of understanding of the tax rules (or working with an undereducated tax accountant)
3. Losing your business

Word of Warning

As you read about the different deductions and ways to reduce your tax liability, be sure not to lose sight of your bigger goal, which is to achieve Prolific Profit. It may be tempting to spend a ton of money to reduce your tax liability, but this strategy is short-sighted if it is pursued as a singular focus. Keep this information in the back of your tool kit and use it as part of your overall profitability strategy. If you're interested in learning about specific tax strategies, feel free to grab the free tax saving resources at ProlificProfit.com or reach out to me so I can do a proper diagnosis and understand your unique situation. I've seen too many scenarios where someone takes information from an online resource or book, carelessly implements the information,

then gets hit with an audit and fines. This is why I'd much rather have a conversation or recommend you speak to a tax professional. Imagine a doctor giving a prescription without getting your medical history and doing a thorough examination. He could kill you! If I don't have any information about your business and life, it would truly be malpractice for me to tell you what to do.

The Purpose of Taxes

Income tax in the United States has evolved greatly since its introduction in 1861. The tax code is over 70,000 pages, and in 2017 it underwent a major overhaul with the Tax Cuts and Jobs Act (TCJA).[24]

Historically, tariffs provided the primary source of revenue for the government. New taxes were often introduced during times of war to raise additional revenue, but they were normally permitted to expire when the war was over. For instance, in order to finance U.S. participation in World War I, Congress passed the 1916 Revenue Act and then the War Revenue Act of 1917. The highest income tax rate jumped from 15 percent in 1916 to 67 percent in 1917 and 77 percent in 1918![25]

Over time the government noticed that they could influence behavior by increasing or decreasing the taxes associated with different activities. My clients and other business owners that legally and ethically pay little-to-no tax do so because they understand that the tax law is a tool the government uses to influence social and economic behavior, not necessarily to raise revenue.

Without this understanding, many business owners wait until the end of the year to talk to their tax accountant to find out how much they owe. Unfortunately, there's only so much even the most advanced tax accountant can do. If taxes are written to influence behavior, your behavior needs to be more aligned with what the government wants you to do, which is evidenced by the facts of the situation. Therefore, if you want to change your tax, you have to change your facts.

---

[24] https://taxfoundation.org/income-tax-code-spans-more-70000-pages/
[25] https://bradfordtaxinstitute.com/Free_Resources/Federal-Income-Tax-Rates.aspx

While there are some tax strategies that can help reduce the tax liability for employees (W-2 workers), the vast majority of taxes benefit business owners and investors. People that are unaware of the purpose of the tax code are outraged by this fact. The truth of the matter is that business owners and investors provide so much economic benefit through employment, housing, and providing capital to businesses that it's in the government's best interest to continue to reward these individuals. As such, I will dedicate the rest of this section to the 78% of business owners who overpay in taxes.

In saying that, I want to make it clear before we go further that there are four tax rules to live by:

1. Follow the tax code and do everything with integrity
2. Everything in tax reduction starts with a goal
3. You need to understand your vision before you can start reducing your tax bill
4. Work with a professional

Four Requirements for Business Deductions

Some specific business tax deductions are spelled out in the IRS tax code, but the vast majority of the tax deductions are not listed. I believe the reason for this is to add some brevity (even though the tax code is over 70,000 pages) and allow taxpayers to use their judgment. To provide guidance to business owners, the IRS provides four basic principles that must be met for a business expense to be considered deductible:

1. The expenses must be incurred in connection with your trade, business, or profession
2. The expenses must be "ordinary"
3. The expenses must be "necessary"

4. The expenses must "not be lavish or extravagant under the circumstances"

If any one of these requirements is not met, the business activity cannot be deducted on your business tax return. To avoid being in the naughty house with the IRS, here's a more in-depth explanation for each of the requirements.

Requirement #1: Business Related

To meet this requirement, the expenses must be incurred in connection with your trade, business, or profession. The IRS wants you to perform these

activities with "a reasonable degree of regularity" and a "sincere attempt to make a profit." This rule not only applies to business owners but also self-employed individuals, independent contractors, freelancers, and part-time entrepreneurs.

"Reasonable degree of regularity" means that your business activity cannot be performed every once in a while, or with minimal effort.

"Sincere attempt to make a profit" means that you must show that the purpose of your business is not just for fun as a hobby, but a business in which you are consciously trying to generate profit. If not, the IRS will classify the business as a hobby, thus classifying what you considered business deductions as personal expenses.

"In connection with your trade or business" means that the business must exist before you can begin writing off business expenses. If you are just thinking of starting a business, researching, or talking about owning a business, this will disqualify your business expenses as well.

Requirement #2: Ordinary Expenses

This requirement relates to what the IRS defines as "ordinary". By the IRS's definition, an ordinary expense is one that is common or accepted in your type of business. This doesn't mean that the expense needs to occur frequently, but it should be a common-sense expense related to your business.

Some commonly overlooked ordinary business expenses include:

- Vehicles (Actual vs. Miles)
- Business Travel
- Meals (the new TCJA disallowed entertainment as a deductible business expense)
- Equipment and Furniture
- Home Office
- Retirement
- Maximizing Depreciation

Requirement #3: Necessary Expenses

A necessary expense, according to the IRS, is one "that is appropriate and helpful in developing and maintaining your trade or business." Part of the requirement is "economic justification" for an expense.

Requirement #4: Not "Lavish or Extravagant"

Business expenses cannot be "lavish or extravagant" based on the facts of the activity. It makes sense for a bigger business with more income to deduct larger expenses. Smaller, part-time entrepreneurs have no business going out on expensive dinners or purchasing expensive vehicles through their business. While there is some gray area in this requirement, try to use your best judgment and steer toward the conservative spectrum.

Deductions vs. Credits

A common question I get from clients is the difference between a deduction and a credit. The short answer is that deductions reduce your taxable income, while credits reduce your tax burden (i.e., the tax you pay).

Deductions

Deductions generally come from your qualified business expenses. If a business expense meets all four requirements, this reduces your taxable income amount, thus providing a lower number that is calculated against your tax rate. For example, say you purchased accounting services (hint, hint, wink, wink), you now know that accounting is the language of business and therefore it is absolutely business-related, ordinary, necessary for your business, and probably the least lavish and extravagant purchase you can make. Say you spend about $2,000 on accounting services and have a business income of $10,000. Assuming you are in a 24% tax bracket, instead of your taxable income being $10,000, it will decrease it to $8,000, thus providing you a tax savings of $480 ($2,000 x 24%).

Deductions can be grouped into two categories: "above the line" deductions and "below the line" deductions (also referred to as "itemized" deductions). Above the line deductions would be your business expenses as well as the higher of itemized deductions of the fixed "standard deduction". As such, you cannot deduct both itemized and standard deductions.

Below is an example of how this would look mathematically:

Total income (sum of all of your income)

-Above the line deductions

= Adjusted gross income "The Line"

-Standard deduction *or* itemized deductions

= Taxable income

Qualified Business Income (QBI)

One of the new tax advantages from TCJA is qualified business income. Many owners of sole proprietorships, partnerships, S corporations, and some trusts and estates may be eligible for a qualified business income (QBI) deduction—also called Section 199A—for tax years beginning after December 31, 2017. The deduction allows eligible taxpayers to deduct up to 20 percent of their qualified business income (QBI), plus 20 percent of qualified real estate investment trust (REIT) dividends and qualified publicly traded partnership (PTP) income. Income earned through a C corporation or by providing services as an employee are not eligible for the deduction.[26]

The deduction is available regardless of whether taxpayers itemize deductions on Schedule A or take the standard deduction. The deduction amount depends on the taxpayer's total taxable income—which includes wages, interest, capital gains, and so on—in addition to income generated by the business. Once the taxable income reaches or exceeds $157,500 ($315,000 if filing jointly), the type of business also comes into play. Once the taxable income threshold has been exceeded, specified service trades or

---

[26] https://www.irs.gov/pub/irs-pdf/p535.pdf

businesses (SSTBs) are excluded. SSTBs are broken into two distinct categories:

1. Trades or businesses performing services in the fields of health, law, accounting, actuarial science, performing arts, consulting, athletics, financial services, brokerage services, or any trade or business where the principal asset of that trade or business is the reputation or skill of one or more of its employees (these fields are listed in Sec. 1202(e)(3)(A); however, the TCJA specifically excluded engineering and architecture);

2. Any trade or business that involves the performance of services that consist of investing and investment management, trading, or dealing in securities described in Sec. 475(c)(2), partnership interests, or commodities described in Sec. 475(e)(2) (Sec. 199A(d)(2)(B)).

Credits

Unlike deductions, credit goes directly against your taxes—dollar for dollar. Say you end up owing $2,500 in taxes and get a tax credit of $2,500 (like an education credit); this directly reduces the amount owed by $2,500, resulting in ZERO taxes owed.

The government creates tax credits to incentivize taxpayers to do something they believe is beneficial for the community. Again, all you have to do is learn the things that the government wants you to do, do them, and then get your

tax credit. Many taxpayers may be getting tax credits without even realizing it. The more aware you are of the different credits available to you, the more you can take advantage of them. This is why I believe that tax credits are one of many amazing tax savings that are out there.

There are two main types of tax credits. The first is a refundable credit. You can receive this credit even in the event that you don't have any taxes due in the first place. In this case, you might completely remove your taxable income through a number of the methods I am sharing in this book and still receive a refund from the government for the sum of the credit.

The other form of tax credits is a nonrefundable credit. You simply get this credit if you actually have taxes due. You can carry some of these credits over to other years, but unfortunately, for many of them, if you don't use them, you lose them. It is critical that you do proper tax planning to know what your taxes will be throughout the year so you can make sure you have enough income to use up the credits.

Reflections & Actions

1. How confident are you that you are taking all of your deductions?

   _____

2. What deductions and credits do you think you're missing out on?

   _____

3. Do you qualify for the QBI deduction? Was this taken on your tax return?

   _____

Go to ProlificProfit.com to download your free full-page colored infographic of Strategies to Taming the Tax Troll.

CHAPTER 15

Asset Vs. Profit Protection - Understanding Entity Structure

B elieve it or not, your legal entity structure could be one of the biggest contributors to your overpayment in taxes. Not only is it important to have the right legal entity from a tax perspective, but it can also be important how you operate your business from the standpoint of legal liabilities. Being sued is a sure-fire way to ruin your operating cash flow, and therefore it is important that you understand the different entity types and how they impact your business. One common misunderstanding among business owners (and I am ashamed to say, some tax accountants) is the difference between a legal entity and tax entity. In short, a legal entity is the entity you register with the state and a tax entity is the entity you "elect" for tax purposes.

Legal Entities vs. Tax Entities

The two most common forms of legal entities in the United States are Corporations and Limited Liability Companies (Limited Partnerships are another form, whereas Professional Limited Liability Companies, Professional Associations, Limited Liability Partnerships, and Limited

Liability Limited Partnerships are usually used for professional purposes (accountants, lawyers, doctors, architects, etc.)). I also wanted to note that "doing business as" (DBA) is not a legal entity and therefore does not give you limited liability or legal protections. It's just a fictitious name used for your business and most often used by sole proprietors.

When speaking to business owners, they'll most likely say they have a corporation, limited liability company, or partnership. The reasons for choosing one over another will be discussed in this chapter, but for now, know they have their own legal requirements and liability protection. Generally, LLCs are easier to deal with and are the newer form of a legal entity. According to the IRS, a Limited Liability Company (LLC) is an entity created by state statute. Depending on elections made by the LLC and the number of members, the IRS will treat an LLC either as a corporation, a partnership, or as part of the owner's tax return (a "disregarded entity"). As such, you cannot be taxed as an LLC.

Another thing to note is that entities in the US are formed on the state level only, and the choice is made with the condition of creation. For legal entities, each state has different laws, so it's best to consult with an attorney to ensure you have the appropriate asset protection.

A tax entity is an election by the business owner deciding on the way the entity wants to be taxed. Most states tax the entity just like the national election, although some states require a state-level election.

In regard to taxes, there are four tax entities to choose from: sole proprietorship (a disregarded entity), partnership, S-corporation, or C-corporation.

Entities	Sole Proprietor	Partnership	S-Corp	C-Corp
Sole Proprietor	Yes	No	No	No
LLC (single member)	Yes	No	Yes	Yes

LLC (multi-member)	No	Yes	Yes	Yes
Partnership	No	Yes	No	No
Corporation	No	No	Yes	Yes

Sole Proprietorship

Sole proprietorships are easy to form when you're starting out, especially if you have no liability problems, no employees, and do not expect to profit more than $50,000 (I'll explain why later). Sole proprietorships are the easiest, lowest-costing entity to run and manage.

Advantages of a Sole Proprietorship

1. Simplicity. As I mentioned, this is the least complicated form of a business entity. There's only one owner, typically no employees, and you are only required to file a Schedule C with your federal Form 1040 tax return. By being a single-owner entity, you have more control over business decisions since you don't have partners or other owners. The costs to start a sole proprietorship are comparably low to the other entities since there are no filings of organizational documents.

2. Pass-through entity. Since sole proprietorships are considered pass-through entities, any losses in the business can be applied towards earnings on your personal return. They also allow you to take advantage of the Qualified Business Income (QBI) deduction if you meet the requirements.

3. Tax Benefits. As a sole proprietorship, you are allowed to deduct certain expenses such as a self-insured medical reimbursement plan if you hire your spouse.

Disadvantages of a Sole Proprietorship

1. Unlimited liability. In the event your business is sued, your personal assets such as your home, vehicle, and cash will be at risk. This risk significantly increases with having employees because either they or the customers they work with can come after you. This is one of the easiest ways to lose your business and it is not worth it for most business owners. Even with general liability insurance, your best bet is to set up a different legal entity structure such as an LLC, S-Corp, or C-Corp.

2. Issues raising capital. Investors typically don't invest in businesses that are sole proprietorships because there is minimal recourse. As a sole proprietorship, your personal assets are the primary collateral and are typically not enough to repay investors.

3. No business continuity. The business typically lives and dies with the owner. If the owner is unable to work because of death or disability, the business will go with him or her.

Partnerships

According to the IRS, a partnership is a relationship existing between two or more persons who join to carry on a trade or business. Each person contributes money, property, labor, or skill and expects to share in the profits and losses of the business.

A partnership must file an annual information return to report the income, deductions, gains, losses, etc., from its operations, but it does not pay income tax. Instead, it "passes through" any profits or losses to its partners. Each partner includes his or her share of the partnership's income or loss on his or her tax return.[27]

Partners are not employees and should not be issued a Form W-2. The partnership must furnish copies of Schedule K-1 (Form 1065) to the partners by the date Form 1065 is required to be filed, including extensions. The Schedule K-1 is a tax form issued annually for an investment in partnership interests. The purpose of the Schedule K-1 is to report each partner's share of the partnership's earnings, losses, deductions, and credits.

There are two forms of partnership: a general partnership and a limited partnership. As a partner, you get taxed on the "tax basis" of your ownership.

Tax basis refers to the amount of money a person has invested in an asset. A partner's basis is increased by the following items:

- The partner's additional contributions to the partnership, including an increased share of, or assumption of, partnership liabilities.
- The partner's distributive share of taxable and nontaxable partnership income.
- The partner's distributive share of the excess of the deductions for depletion over the basis of the depletable property, unless the property is oil or gas wells whose basis has been allocated to partners.[28]

---

[27] https://www.irs.gov/businesses/small-businesses-self-employed/partnerships
[28] https://www.irs.gov/businesses/small-businesses-self-employed/partnerships

Advantages of a Partnership

1. More opportunities to raise capital. Since there are more owners in a partnership, there is more collateral to put up, thus making it easier to get a loan and investors. Even though it is not the ideal entity to attract investors, it's one step above a sole proprietor.

2. Lower complexity. Generally, partnerships are simple to form. Partnerships need a partnership agreement to outline the partnership relationship. There are few filings with the IRS and state, which results in lower costs.

3. Pass-through entity. Partnerships are also considered pass-through entities; any losses in the business can be applied towards earnings on your personal return. This also allows you to take advantage of the Qualified Business Income (QBI) deduction if you meet the requirements.

Disadvantages of Partnership

1. Lack of continuity. Like sole proprietorships, partnerships are terminated if a partner dies, retires, withdrawals, or resigns. This rule can be overcome by including in your partnership agreement that the partnership will not terminate if there is a death, disability, or withdrawal of a partner.

2. Self-employment taxes. A partner's share of the ordinary income reported on a Schedule K-1 is subject to the self-employment tax. This is a 15.3% tax (social security and Medicare) on all profits generated by the business that are not exempt from these taxes.

3. Unlimited liability. Just like sole proprietors, you're personally liable for any lawsuits against your partnership. To make matters worse, you're unlimitedly liable for the actions of your partners and for all partnership debts (unless they are specifically nonrecourse debts).

C Corporations

By definition, a corporation is a company or group of people authorized to act as a single entity (legally a person) and recognized as such in law. Incorporating means "to create a separate body" that can borrow money, be responsible for debts, and run a business.

Advantages of a C Corporation

1. Limited liability. Corporations provide limited liability as long as the owners adhere to the rules specific to corporations. By failing to adhere to the corporation's formalities, committing fraud, or malpractice, you can lose this asset protection. Unlike partnerships, the partner who committed malpractice will be held personally liable for this action. The other owners in the corporation will not be personally liable, thus limiting their liability.

2. Lower tax rate. As a result of the new tax laws, the C corporation tax rate is now a flat 21 percent.

3. Fringe benefits. C corporations and employees of S-corporations who own less than 2 percent of the stock are allowed to take advantage of several fringe benefits. If you're not aware, a fringe benefit is an extra benefit supplementing an employee's salary, for example, a company car, subsidized meals, health insurance, etc.

Many of these provide tax deductions that can significantly reduce your tax liability.

4. Longevity. The entity continues to exist beyond the deaths of the owners.

5. Great for raising capital. It is easier to attract capital with the sale of stocks and bonds. A corporation can have an unlimited number of investors.

Disadvantages of a C Corporation

1. Double taxation. The corporation pays federal and state taxes on its profits. This makes sense since C Corporations are treated as separate entities. By being an owner of the C Corporation, you can be double taxed, once with the entity, second at your dividend tax rate. Some of this can be reduced with proper tax planning.

2. Costly. As a C Corporation, you must file a separate corporate tax return along with schedules such as Form 1120. Additionally, as an employee of the corporation, you must file both the federal and state documentation such as an Employer Identification Number (EIN) along with the entity set up, which will include attorney fees.

3. Rules, rules, rules. As a C Corporation, there are several requirements that must be met to maintain your entity status. As a C Corporation, you must have yearly stockholder meetings to elect a board of directors, yearly board meetings to elect officers, and documented meetings throughout the year for major issues and decisions within the corporation. Failure to meet these rules (and several others) will "pierce the corporate veil," meaning that you will be held personally liable for corporate debts and obligations.

States require the filing of the Articles of Incorporation, corporate bylaws, and annual reports. Corporations that have assets of $10 million or more and file at least 250 returns annually are required to electronically file their Forms 1120 and 1120S for tax years ending on or after December 31, 2007.[29]

4. No pass-through. Unlike the other entities previously mentioned, losses from the corporation stay in the corporation. Therefore you cannot apply losses from the corporation against your personal income.

S Corporations

An S corporation is a corporation with some special tax treatments. Since it is a corporation, it has the exact same formalities as a regular corporation such as stockholder meetings and board of directors' meetings, etc. Additionally, as an S Corp, you must make a tax election by filing Form 2553 with the IRS within the first 75 days of the tax year if you want to operate as an S corporation for the year. If you don't do this, you may be treated as a C corporation.

Advantages of an S Corporation

1. Limited liability. As with some of the entities we discussed, an S corporation protects the personal assets of its shareholders.

2. Pass-through entity. Unlike C corporations, an S corporation does not pay federal taxes at the corporate level. As such, any business income or loss is "passed-through" to the owner's personal

---

[29] https://www.irs.gov/businesses/small-businesses-self-employed/forming-a-corporation

income tax returns, allowing business losses to be offset with personal income.

3. Tax-benefits. One of the biggest advantages of owning an S corporation is the elimination of up to 50 percent of your Social Security and Medicare taxes with the use of S Corporation dividends.[30] You can really maximize this benefit if you make less than the Social Security maximum, which is $128,400 in 2018.

Disadvantages of an S Corporation

1. More rules. According to the IRS, to qualify for S corporation status, the corporation must meet the following requirements:

- Be a domestic corporation
- Have only allowable shareholders:
  - o May be individuals, certain trusts, and estates and
  - o May not be partnerships, corporations or non-resident alien shareholders
- Have no more than 100 shareholders
- Have only one class of stock
- Not be an ineligible corporation (i.e., certain financial institutions, insurance companies, and domestic international sales corporations).[31]

2. Failure to comply with any of these requirements and you lose your S corporation status the day you violate the requirement.

3. Limited fringe benefits. Even though an S corporation is a form of a corporation, they do not get many of the fringe benefits a C Corporation

---

[30] Sections 61, 3121(a), 3306(b), Revenue Ruling 73-361, 1973-2 CB 331.
[31] https://www.irs.gov/businesses/small-businesses-self-employed/forming-a-corporation

would get such as medical reimbursement plans. As such, most fringe benefits provided by the corporation are taxable as compensation to employee-shareholders who own more than 2 percent of the corporation.

4. More challenging to raise capital. Due to the limits of shareholders (less than 100), S corporation cannot get as many shareholders as a C Corporation.

As you can imagine, each tax entity has different tax forms and treatment. Below is a quick overview of the different categories:

	Sole Prop	Partnership	LLC	S-Corp	C-Corp
Tax Forms	1099	1065/K-1	Depends	1120S/K-1/ W-2	1120/W-2
Pass-Through	Yes	Yes	Depends	Yes	No
Self-Employment	Yes	Yes	Depends	No	No

Go to ProlificProfit.com to download your free full-page colored infographic of Asset vs Profit Protection.

Recordkeeping Considerations

When running a business, good record keeping is important. As I've discussed throughout this book, maintaining detailed records helps you more accurately monitor how well your company is doing. Records allow you to determine which expenses should be cut, which expenditures are

producing results, which customers are your most profitable, etc. Recordkeeping is also vital for tax purposes.

It makes the job a lot easier for the individual preparing your taxes, whether you are doing it yourself or getting expert help. If you are audited and can't produce evidence of the expenses you claimed as a deduction, the deduction is likely to be disallowed. There are lots of recordkeeping software products (e.g., QuickBooks, Xero) that are both affordable and fairly easy to use. The financial risk you incur by not maintaining documents far exceeds the price of these applications.

The first step, if you have not done so already, is to have a business checking account. The main record of maintaining is a ledger. This is a record of all your business transactions. You will find paper versions at office supply shops, but it is a fantastic idea to find software that will assist you with this. For those just starting out, a simple spreadsheet program can do the job.

However, should you use a software package to assist you, make sure you backup your document regularly. Losing this information because of something as easy as a computer failure will not be a good enough excuse for the IRS. For tax purposes, you'll also have to keep supporting documents for your ledger. For your income, these can be matters such as invoices, bank deposit slips, etc. (If you operate a business with a lot of cash sales, it is important to maintain a daily log of the total amount of money received.) For expenses, you need to have the ability to prove two things: That the money was spent on something that qualifies as a deduction, and that you are the

person who spent the money. This means that neither a receipt (which demonstrates exactly what the money was spent on) or a credit card invoice (which proves that you are the person who spent the money) may be sufficient.

Reflections & Actions

1. What is your legal entity?

_____

2. What is your tax entity?

_____

3. Do you believe you could benefit from switching entities?

_____

PART III

ACCOUNTABILITY

CHAPTER 16

The Prolific Professional

O ne of my favorite quotes comes from Uncle Ben in the movie *Spider-Man*, who tells Peter Parker (Spider-Man) is that "with great power comes great responsibility." At the moment, Peter did not truly understand the importance of this lesson until after (spoiler alert!)... Ben was killed. As Spider-Man later discovers, the killer of his uncle was a thief he purposely let escape. If Peter had not ignored his responsibility as a web-slinging hero, he

could've stopped the thief and his Uncle Ben would have still been alive.

Given everything we went over in the previous section (which was a lot), you now have the power to be the hero of your businesses—and possibly the world. As this hero, it is your responsibility to ensure you're taking the required actions to ensure you achieve Prolific Profit. I have given these heroes a name, which I call the Prolific Professional.

The Prolific Professional doesn't wear a mask or a cape (with the exception of Halloween or maybe with a significant other, not judging), and on the outside they may look more like Clark Kent than Superman. But don't let that fool you—the Prolific Professional is an individual committed to achieving their Prolific Purpose through a high degree of accountability and intense focus on improving results. These results are reflected through profits, operating cash, and/or impact on the world.

KPIs: The Super Power of the Prolific Professional

One of your superpowers is the knowledge of key performance indicators (KPIs). KPIs are commonly described as a quantifiable measure used to evaluate the success of an organization, employee, and so on. Essentially, a KPI is created to measure the activity of a particular aspect of the organization and helps break down the success factors by certain activities or departments. This helps everyone understand the goals that need to be achieved and exactly what metric will be measured to determine the success or failure of meeting that goal.

Business is simply cause and effect. I've shared some financial KPIs throughout this book, and with this knowledge you can measure the effect (the results) and change the cause (activities). As I've mentioned, being big isn't the same as being Prolific. We've seen hundreds of "big" companies collapse over the past decades such as Enron, Circuit City, Blockbuster, Toys "R" Us, and many others.

Succeeding in business requires you to be nimble and adaptable. Part of this is making sure you're not being dragged down by unnecessary expenses, but the bigger part of it is knowing where you are with your KPIs and working relentlessly towards improving those metrics. You may be an "LLC" or bringing in money, but that doesn't mean you're in business. Many illegitimate businesses (which I call "bidness") or struggling businesses still make money, but the truly successful businesses are run by someone that is obsessed with metrics.

In fact, all the true master's in business—Jeff Bezos (Amazon), Warren Buffet (Berkshire Hathaway), Steve Jobs (Apple), and Phil Knight (Nike), to name a few—are obsessed with results. These business geniuses are constantly measuring, reviewing, and improving their results. Even the slightest deviation from projections may trigger a violent response because they understand the snowball impact of getting off course. As the widely respected management consultant Peter Drucker says, "What gets measured gets managed."

To be a Prolific Professional, you must apply this same level of intensity to your business. If you're not measuring, how are you going to improve your results? How do you even know *what* to improve? I can admit that this is not the easiest thing to do, especially if your business has been struggling for a while. What makes a business owner a Prolific Professional comes down to their behavior.

I liken it to the straight-A student in elementary school. They love getting their report card because it's an opportunity to celebrate in glee and be shown love from their parents. Any deviation from the A is devastating for the straight-A student (trust me, I know—my sister was a straight-A student). As a result of the deviation, that student will analyze the semester and take the necessary action required to improve their grades. Meanwhile, the D and F

students are finding every excuse in the world to avoid coming home to their parents. They will run, hide, lie, and cheat, whatever they need to do to avoid dealing with their results—everything, that is, except make the necessary changes to improve.

It's easy to see the parallel to your business. Your KPIs shine a floodlight on your activities. If your activities were good, your numbers will be good; if your activities were not so good, your numbers will be bad. Just like Superman's ability to fly or Batman's ability to...drive cool cars, your KPIs are only worthwhile if you use them for good. Once you see a KPI, you must take action to improve that result. Measuring KPIs is the difference between business and "bidness".

Reflections & Actions

1. Are you a Prolific Professional?

_____

2. How well have you been tracking your metrics?

_____

3. What can you do today to become completely obsessed with metrics?

_____

CHAPTER 17

Tapping Into Your Superpower

We've covered a lot of KPIs and metrics in this book, and you may be feeling overwhelmed. This is completely normal, and it's actually a good thing because it means you're growing. As a refresher, I would like to share a couple of best practices as they relate to KPIs.

1. Consider all factors when reviewing your KPIs: For instance, if you're looking to increase Accounts Receivable, then you might see your disputed payment rate. You may determine that the cause of the increase is because the business is growing exponentially.

2. Don't neglect qualitative factors: Employee satisfaction may result in higher performance, which can in turn result in higher earnings and profit. Employees should be motivated to work towards your Prolific Purpose and mission. Financial incentives and rewards may be a good way to push employees to get results.

3. Get buy-in from your team: From the intern to the supervisors, your team needs to be on the same page when it comes to your KPIs. Remember, this is a non-negotiable component of running your business. Keep KPIs top of mind by putting them on a whiteboard and sharing overall results with your team. If you have people that are not on the same page, then you need to let them go.

In the previous chapters, I discussed some basic strategies to enhance your metrics, but as a business owner, you're accountable for identifying more KPIs for your specific company and communicating those to your group.

Reviewing Your KPIs

While it's good to establish goals and KPIs, the most critical factor for success is to have some form of accountability to keep those KPIs on track and hit those targets. In other words, you need to "INSPECT WHAT YOU EXPECT." This is why I strongly recommend an end-of-day (EOD) recap.

Here's how it works: Every day, take 10-15 minutes to assess what happened that day and whether you are on track to reaching your objectives. You must identify where you stand in regard to your key metrics and exactly what occurred throughout the day to make those metrics go down or up. From the report, ask yourself:

- What can we improve tomorrow?
- What will be the top priority jobs?
- What is the status of each activity?

When you're ready to build your own EOD Recap Report, head over to ProlificProfit.com to download the template.

Now that you're clear on the best way to review what happened every day as it pertains to your KPIs, I will now switch gears and concentrate on getting you to your Prolific Purpose in the mornings as well. While the EOD recap is excellent to review, you also need to be proactive rather than merely reflective. Having a Morning Check-In Report gets you clear on your objectives for the day and reorganizes your ideas around the KPIs you've set for yourself, your company, and your life.

Each morning take 10-15 minutes to examine what the day will look like and where your priorities lie. You might also want to do a mid-afternoon checkup to keep on top of your objectives throughout the day.

Head to ProlificProfit.com to pull on the Morning Check-In Report.

Determine the Root Causes

Now that you've identified which metrics are the most significant to track your success, what do you do if you *don't* see success? Here are some common issues:

1. *Not seeing the link between your KPIs and your Prolific Purpose.* We aren't just going through the motions of constructing KPIs for the pleasure of it. Rather, they should assist you in achieving the goals you've outlined from the Clarity section. If you aren't clear on the reason or the intention behind a KPI you've set, return to your goals and ask yourself whether it relates to some of these. If you cannot find a reason, just do away with it.

2. *Not being able to quantify the KPI success.* If you've created KPIs outside of the financial metrics I've shared in this book, or if you can't tell if you're WINNING or FAILING in your KPI, then you need to reevaluate what KPI you're using in the first place. A fantastic instance of this is Client Support. If you aren't utilizing a platform where your customers can rank your answers, then you don't know whether your clients are miserable or vice versa.

3. *Improper incentives for KPIs.* A great example of this is the Accounts Receivable collections group. Let's say you would like your staff to boost collections to 85 percent, so you inform them they will get a 1 percent bonus for their efforts during the week. Your staff starts to call clients to collect aggressively on the outstanding payments, and AR collection rate starts increase, but client retention and satisfaction both decline. You then find out that the decline in retention and satisfaction has happened because your staff has been rude to your customers, and a few of your team members have even made threats to your customers claiming they will report their accounts to credit bureaus if they don't receive payment immediately. By improperly incentivizing your staff to increase collection rates without training them on the most effective way to do so, they will likely take it upon themselves to meet this KPI their own way.

At the end of the day, KPIs help show you whether things are moving in the ideal direction and (hopefully) provide you ample time to make any necessary adjustments. Listed below are a couple of things to keep in the back of your mind when analyzing your metrics:

- Do they link to my Prolific Purpose?
- Are they easy and easy to comprehend?
- Are they applicable to my own needs, and if not, what's the procedure to update/change them?
- Do they concentrate on feedback and improvement for those parties involved?
- Are they really going to help me or my company?

Reflections & Actions

1. What exactly does KPI stand for?

   _____

2. List out a couple of KPIs you have heard of before reading this book:

   _____

3. List the #1 KPI you will begin to track in your company.

   _____

4. What should you do if your KPI is at the FAIL standing?

   _____

5. When do you intend to perform your End of Day Recap?

   _____

6. List an important KPI challenge you will bear in mind.

   _____

7. What KPI do you want to find out more about and execute in your personal or business life?

   _____

CHAPTER 18

Victory Lap

———————o———————

You've come a long way, and as we approach the end of this book, I want to reinforce some of the principles we've covered thus far. Imagine that your goals have likely changed (if not, re-read this book!). Whether it's a newfound appreciation for the language of business, key metrics, the alchemy of business, taming taxes, hiring a Profit Producing Professional, or why you MUST achieve Prolific Profits, the principles from this book will fundamentally change the way you approach your business. Consider this your victory lap.

Revised Goal Setting: Out with the Old, In with the New

Remember back in the Clarity section when you developed new goals based on where you currently stood and where you wanted to go? Now that you've been given all this new information about maximizing profits and dominating the market, take some time to assess whether or not these goals have changed.

When you come across new information, it often changes what you think you wanted and what you thought you were capable of achieving. Let's revisit the

goals you set for yourself in the Clarity section and ask yourself: Did the specific goal change now that you're at the end of the book?

1. When do you plan on retiring? Old Goal

   _____

   New Goal

   _____

2. How much money do you want to have when you retire? Old Goal

   _____

   New Goal

   _____

3. Where do you want to live when you retire? Old Goal

   _____

   New Goal

   _____

4. At retirement age, what do you want to be doing each day? Old Goal

   _____

   New Goal

   _____

5. What do you want your most successful achievement to be by the time you retire?

   Old Goal

   _____

New Goal

_____

List Out 10 NEW Personal Goals (Do Not Have To Be Financial):

1.

_____

2.

_____

4.

_____

5.

_____

6.

_____

7.

_____

8.

_____

9.

_____

10.

_____

List Out 10 NEW Business Goals (Do Not Have To Be Financial):

1.

_____

2.

_____

3.

_____

4.

_____

5.

_____

6.

_____

7.

_____

8.

_____

9.

_____

10.

_____

Now that you have reviewed your goals…did they change?

When it comes to goal setting, you want to make sure that you are constantly reviewing and acknowledging your stated goals and adjusting them based on changes that happen in your life.

Just like with the GPS, if you decide halfway through driving to New York City that you would rather visit California, you can easily switch your destination and put yourself on the path towards Los Angeles.

Building Your Monthly and Yearly Projections: It's All in the Plan

We've discussed goal setting early on, and as you can see, it is a crucial component of success. When you envision a goal and put a plan in place to get there, it significantly increases your chances of hitting your goal—much more so than if you simply hope to fall on your goal by mere happenstance.

Once you determine the end game and set your goals, you need to map out a plan to get there.

- How many sales/net profits do you need each year from now until you retire to meet your goals?
- What marketing structure or customer base do you need and how many leads do you need to generate to achieve your sales targets?
- Are there additional hires needed to get to the numbers you need to reach?

All of these questions should be asked and analyzed to help steer you toward your intended goal.

Year-by-Year Breakdown of Your Desires

There is a stigma in our culture where we are not allowed to express what we truly want. Our culture tends to look negatively on people who talk about what they want, especially when those wants are financial or material. In the early sections of this book, you put down several high-level goals. Let's revisit them now.

Remember how the power of visualization can help you bring the future into the present? The future is first created in the mind, so the bigger you imagine, the bigger your present will become. Ask yourself what your life will look like and feel free to mention the following or anything else that comes to mind:

- Where will you live?
- How much will you make?
- What will you be doing with your time?
- What possessions will you own?
- What activities will you have done/participated in?
- Anything else that comes to mind?

CHAPTER 19

Hiring A Profit-Producing Professional And Next Steps

---

opefully, you've been able to see the value a great Profit-Producing Professional (PPP) can bring to you your business. A PPP is your secret weapon to maximizing profits and dominating your market. You now have the knowledge necessary to identify a true PPP and quickly spot a lousy accountant. While PPPs do not just give their time away, you do not need to pay an arm and a leg to hire a great PPP. It's not only an investment in your business, but your life. To recap, some of the value-added services of a PPP include, but are not limited to:

- Proactive tax planning
- Maximizing profits through revenue and cost analysis
- Identifying key performance indicators (KPIs) and mapping out reports to monitor them
- Ongoing reporting and financial analysis prepared for the company
- Interpreting financial results on an ongoing basis
- Coordination with onsite bookkeepers and accounting staff
- Creation of training for accounting staff and other company members
- Recommendations of new technology to aid in objectives (and potential implementation)
- Cash management, forecasting, and planning

- Managing annual budgeting & forecasting process
- Participating in board meetings
- Participating in meetings with potential investors
- Deal analysis for mergers and acquisitions
- Representing you in front of the IRS

While this list may seem overwhelming, you should be excited by the growth your business will experience partnering with a PPP, which brings us to the conclusion of this book. It cannot be stressed enough that your primary goal as a business owner is to achieve the highest level of Hierarchy of Business Success by converting assets to free cash flow through the CPA Success System. I provided you with several strategies in order to do this. This book should be used as a reference, and I encourage you to read it several times. As you continue to climb up the Hierarchy of Business Success, you will face new challenges and will gain a new perspective by going through the material again and again.

Needless to say, in order to be truly successful in business, you can't go on this journey alone. I'm here to support and deliver value to you every step of the way. Connect with me through email, social media, and be sure to go to ProlificProfit.com to download all your bonuses and get the latest tips and tricks to achieving Prolific Profit. If there's anything I can do to help you, please let me know.

Prolific Postlude: My Gift to Life

Dear Prolific Professional,

I want to acknowledge your openness and commitment to finishing this book. As I've shared many times, this information is simple, but not easy. I've seen countless businesses succeed (and fail) as a result of the principles shared in the book. If there's one thing I want you to take away from this book, it is this: your work, your business, and your Prolific Purpose are *important*. Marian Wright Edelman once said, "Service is the rent we pay for being. It is the very purpose of life, and not something you do in your spare time." As you continue to dedicate your time and valuable service to the world, apply these lessons, dominate your market, and pursue your Prolific Purpose. If you enjoyed this book, share it with a friend. If you hated this book, give it to your worst enemy—they'll thank you for it!

In all seriousness, I'm truly grateful that I was able to share some of my knowledge with you. Whether or not we decide to work together, I take great joy in knowing that this book came across your path.

This is my gift to life.

Your Profit Producing Professional,

Michel Valbrun, CPA, "Money Makin' Mich"

Glossary

Accountability: the fact or condition of being accountable; responsibility. Accountant: a person whose job is to keep or inspect financial accounts. Accounts Receivable: money owed to a company by its debtors.

Accrual Accounting: measures the performance and position of a company by recognizing economic events regardless of when cash transactions occur.

Affirmations: positive statements that can help you to challenge and overcome self-sabotaging and negative thoughts.

Asset: a useful or valuable thing, person, or quality.

Balance Sheet: a statement of the financial position of a business that lists the assets, liabilities and owner's equity at a particular point in time.

Bankruptcy: a legal process through which people or other entities who cannot repay debts to creditors may seek relief from some or all of their debts.

Bean Counter: a person, typically an accountant or bureaucrat, perceived as placing excessive emphasis on controlling expenditure and budgets.

Boogeyman: a person or thing that is widely regarded as an object of fear.

Bookkeeper: a person whose job is to keep records of the financial affairs of a business.

Books records in which all financial information (transactions) of a business or an entity is recorded and maintained.

C.P.A. Success System: the ultimate success system used by Profit Producing Professionals to provide clarity, power, and accountability to business owners.

Cash flow: the total amount of money being transferred into and out of a business, especially as affecting liquidity.

Cash-basis accounting: a method of recording accounting transactions for revenue and expenses only when the corresponding cash is received, or payments are made.

Certified Public Accountant (CPA): a person who is an accounting professional who has passed the Uniform CPA examination and has also met additional state certification and experience requirements.

Clarity: the quality of being coherent and intelligible.

Corporation: a company or group of people authorized to act as a single entity (legally a person) and recognized as such in law.

Cost center: a department or function within an organization that does not directly add to profit but still costs the organization money to operate.

Credit: an entry made on the right side of an account. It either increases equity, liability, or revenue accounts or decreases an asset or expense account.

DBA: "doing business as." It's also referred to as your business's assumed, trade, or fictitious name.

Debit: an accounting entry that either increases an asset or expense account or decreases a liability or equity account.

Deductions: any item or expenditure subtracted from gross income to reduce the amount of income subject to income tax. It is also referred to as an "allowable deduction.

Effectiveness: doing the right things for the business - acquiring and converting assets to revenues.

Effectiveness Ratio: used to analyze how well a company uses its assets and liabilities internally.

Efficiency: doing things right (converting revenues to profit).

Efficiency Ratio: typically used to analyze how well a company uses its assets and liabilities internally.

Enrolled Agent (EA): a person who is a federally-authorized tax practitioner empowered by the U.S. Department of the Treasury.

Financing Cash Flow: section of a company's cash flow statement, which shows the net flows of cash that are used to fund the company. Financing activities include transactions involving debt, equity, and dividends.

Focus: the state or quality of having or producing clear visual definition.

GAAP: is a collection of commonly-followed accounting rules and standards for financial reporting. The acronym is pronounced "gap." GAAP specifications include definitions of concepts and principles, as well as industry-specific rules.

Income Statement: one of the three important financial statements used for reporting a company's financial performance over a specific accounting period.

Investing Cash Flow (ICF): section of a company's cash flow statement that displays how much money has been used in (or generated from) making investments in a specific time period.

IRS (Internal Revenue Service): is the revenue service of the United States federal government.

KPI (Key Performance Indicator): a quantifiable measure used to evaluate the success of an organization, employee, etc. in meeting objectives for performance.

Legal Entities: an individual, company, or organization that has legal rights and obligations.

Liability: as the future sacrifices of economic benefits that the entity is obliged to make to other entities as a result of past transactions or other past events, the settlement of which may result in the transfer or use of assets, provision of services or other yielding of economic benefits in the future.

Limiting Beliefs: are beliefs which constrain us in some way.

LLC (Limited Liability Company): is the US-specific form of a private limited company. It is a business structure that can combine the pass-through taxation of a partnership or sole proprietorship with the limited liability of a corporation.

Luca Pacioli: was an Italian mathematician, Franciscan friar, collaborator with Leonardo da Vinci, and an early contributor to the field now known as accounting.

Michel's Hierarchy of Business Success: a business theory comprising a five-tier model of business success, depicted as hierarchical levels within a pyramid. From the bottom of the hierarchy upwards, the needs are: suicidal, struggling/start-up, stabilized, surplus, and success.

Money Makin' Mich: quintessential Profit Producing Professional.

Operating Cash Flow: a measure of the amount of cash generated by a company's normal business operations.

Operating Cash Flow Ratio: a liquidity ratio, is a measure of how well a company can pay off its current liabilities.

Partnership: a form of business entity involving two or more owners. A partnership is not taxed as a separate entity (though it does file an "informational" tax return) and all profits and losses "flow through" from the partnership to the individual partners and must be included in the individual owners' returns.

Pass-through: entities are not subject to income tax. Rather, the owners are directly taxed individually on the income, taking into account their share of the profits and losses.

Power: ability to do or act; capability of doing or accomplishing something. Productivity: output and input - converting profits to cash.

Productivity Ratio: describe how effectively business assets are deployed.

Profit: excess of revenue over cost is the sum of two components: normal profit and economic profit.

Profit Center: a part of a business which is expected to make an identifiable contribution to the organization's profits.

Profit Producing Professional: an accountant who actively increases profits for a company.

Profitability Ratio: are financial metrics used by analysts and investors to measure and evaluate the ability of a company to generate income (profit) relative to revenue, balance sheet assets.

Prolific: present in large numbers or quantities; plentiful. Prolific Beliefs: abundant empowering beliefs.

Prolific Professional: is an individual committed to achieving their Prolific Purpose through a high degree of accountability and intense focus to improve results. These results are reflected through your profits, operating cash, or impact on the world.

Prolific Profit: the ability to generate an abundant amount of wealth for your business which will lead to market domination.

Prolific Purpose: abundant cause.

Qualified Business Income (QBI): the net amount of qualified items of income, gain, deduction and loss from any qualified trade or business, including income from partnerships, S corporations, sole proprietorships, and certain trusts.

Recordkeeping: the process of recording transactions and events in an accounting system.

Revenue: is the income that a business has from its normal business activities, usually from the sale of goods and services to customers.

S-Corporation: for United States federal income tax, is a closely held corporation that makes a valid election to be taxed under Subchapter S of Chapter 1 of the Internal Revenue Code.

Sole Proprietor: also known as a sole trader, individual entrepreneurship or proprietorship, is a type of enterprise that is owned and run by one person and in which there is no legal distinction between the owner and the business entity.

Stabilized: breakeven in an expanding economy. Risk of operating at a loss.

Statement of Cash Flows: a financial statement that shows how changes in balance sheet accounts and income affect cash and cash equivalents, and breaks the analysis down to operating, investing, and financing activities.

Struggling/Startup: experience of losses and inconsistent cash flow or first year in business. Risk of facing bankruptcy.

Success: profitable in ALL economies.

Suicidal: consistent losses and negative cash flow with minimal opportunity to recover. Inability to pay expenses and debts. Likely to face bankruptcy.

Surplus: profitable in an expanding economy.

Tax Cuts and Jobs Acts (TCJA): passed in December 2017, made several significant changes to the individual income tax.

Tax Entities: an individual or a business that must file a tax return and pay income tax on earnings.

Tax Planning: analysis of a financial situation or plan from a tax perspective. The purpose of tax planning is to ensure tax efficiency. Through tax planning, all elements of the financial plan work together in the most tax-efficient manner possible.

Tax Preparer: a person who calculates, files, and signs income tax returns on behalf of individuals and businesses.

Tax Preparation: the process of preparing tax returns.

Taxes: a compulsory contribution to state revenue, levied by the government on workers' income and business profits, or added to the cost of some goods, services, and transactions.

Value ladder: a method of mapping out your product/service offering visually in ascending order of value and price.

Visualization: the formation of a mental image of something.

INDEX

Victory Lap, v, 131

vision board, 54

Visualization, 53, 146

W

Warning, 99

Warren, 8, 31, 42, 123

Washington, 54

Will, 54, 88

William, 30

Winfrey, 54

Y

Year-by-Year Breakdown, 136

Acknowledgments

To my wife, Racquel, thank you for being such a big part of my growth as a man. Without you, I would not be the person I am today. To my mother and aunt, for raising me and instilling the values of faith and education. To my sisters for always believing in me and supporting me whenever possible. To my clients, thank you for entrusting me to serve you. To my team and business partners, thank you for your dedication and for helping me spread my Prolific Purpose with the world. I truly appreciate all you do! My many mentors, coaches, and teachers thank you for growing my mindset and skills. And to all my extended family and friends (shoutouts to the *Smoov Brothas!*), those who have supported any of my endeavors, attended my workshops, viewed, liked, followed, and commented on any of my content. The late and great Nipsey Hussle, the marthaton continues. Thanks for being an important part of my vision. Without you, I could not maximize my full potential.

Made in the USA
Coppell, TX
14 January 2022

71610441R00094